MW01088313

RV
Boondocking
Basics

© 2016 Yellow Cat Publishing™

All rights reserved, including the right of reproduction in whole or in part in any form.

Yellow Cat and the accompanying logo are registered trademarks owned by Yellow Cat Publishing.

www.yellowcatbooks.com

Names, characters, places, and incidents either are the product of the author's imagination or are used fictitiously. Any resemblance to actual persons, living or dead, events, or locales is entirely coincidental.

• A L S O   B Y   S U N N Y   S K Y E

Living the Simple RV Life

RVing with Pets

The Truth about the RV Life

Tales of a Campground Host

• F O R •

All who love the freedom of the wilds

Contents

Preface

Of all the paths you take in life,
make sure a few of them are dirt. —John Muir

As I write this, I'm camped in the desert near the spectacular and somewhat alien-looking Kofu Mountains of southern Arizona. My little fiberglass trailer is comfy and cozy, but the winds here can be fierce, a fact I experienced firsthand last night.

My small trailer rocked for hours as a cold front came through, in spite of it being hitched to my vehicle with the stabilizers down, techniques that will usually reduce swaying. At times, I imagined I was in a little white rocket about to take off, thrusters roaring. When the winds got especially fierce, I asked myself what I was doing here, wondering if maybe it was time to get a motel room.

But now, as I lean back in my camp chair and drink my freshly made coffee, the winds are gone, and the dark sky is beginning to show the first hints of dawn. The sparkling constellations will soon go to bed as golden rays of sunlight push over the horizon. The temperature is a balmy 60 degrees, even though it's January. If I'd gotten that motel room, I would have missed all this.

And as I sit here, dogs at my feet, listening to a distant lone coyote howl, I think about my life as a full-time boondocker, a life I've led for many years.

Boondocking literally means to "dock" in the "boonies," camping on your own away from RV parks, in a sweeping desert playa or a mountain meadow, free to howl at the moon, run around in your BVDs, or just read your book in peace and quiet with no one around.

Now, as the distant mountains are blanketed with alpenglow, this beautiful sunrise more than makes up for my restless night. I can catch up on my sleep later, and the grandeur all around fills me with a sense of gratitude for the life I lead.

Such are the joys of boondocking, camping off-grid on public lands, far from the crowds, with your only neighbors coyotes and cacti, or maybe coyotes and a mountain stream. To me, this is the definition of freedom—being able to come and go where you want, unhindered and carefree, enjoying the solitude of the natural world.

But not far from where I'm camped are literally hundreds of thousands of RVers, also boondocking, though their experience is much different than mine. It's the winter gathering in Quartzite, where huge crowds of RVers converge to socialize and shop the Big Tent and other attractions, camping cheek to cheek, some in rigs that would outdo many homes for comfort and luxury.

Because they don't have hookups, they'll tell you they're boondocking, but to me, that's not really what the word means. Some will tell you that any time you're without hookups, even if you're in what some call "Camp Walmart," you're boondocking. But I believe there's much more to it than that.

True boondocking means escaping all the hassles that go with civilization while enjoying the freedom of the wilds. And boondocking also means you're self-sufficient, but with the comforts and security one needs. And by definition, boondocking is always free.

For some RVers, recreational parks and campgrounds are exactly what they want and need. There, they have a sense of security, as well as electric, water, and sewer hookups, with clubhouses and amenities like laundromats and organized activities. They can have their air conditioner, their flat-screen TV, and everything else they would have at home, just on a smaller scale. Some even have their own little yards and flower gardens.

But RV parks and campgrounds also have, by necessity, plenty of rules and regulations, and I suspect that running around in your BVDs might be frowned upon. Add to that the sounds and activities of campgrounds: people talking late around smoky campfires, generators, kids yelling, dogs barking, and everything else that goes with people trying to live and have fun in close quarters.

To me, boondocking is exactly the opposite—freedom from irritating people, from rules and regulations, and from watching your hard-earned money disappear as campground fees get higher and higher, not to mention more restrictive (try getting into some of the "nicer" parks with a vintage RV or with pets).

Boondocking is a way to truly get away from it all, and it's not for the timid, nor for those who like lots of human company (although there are groups of boondockers who travel together). It's an exercise in self-sufficiency and hardiness, and there may be times when you get a little nervous over those black clouds on the horizon (don't forget your weather radio) and wonder what to do if you should get stuck, but in general, it's less nerve-wracking than trying to keep from killing the guy parked 10 feet away who's running his generator at 5 a.m.

Being able to successfully live off-grid can open a whole new way of life. Self-sufficiency creates a sense of competency through knowing that you can take care of yourself, which is invaluable not just while camping but throughout life in general.

But of course, like everything else on our beautiful planet, boondocking has its pros and cons. Having spent many years camping on public lands primarily in the western U.S. and Canada, I'd like to explore these pros and cons, and I'm hoping you can avoid my mistakes by learning from my experiences.

It's my hope that by reading this book, those of you who have never boondocked will be encouraged to give it a try. And for those of you who are seasoned boondockers, I hope this book can give you some tips and techniques to make your off-grid experiences even better.

Please note that this is not a book about whether you should become a full-time RVer or not—I address these issues in my other books, Living the Simple RV Life, The Truth About the RV Life, Tales of a Campground Host, and RVing with Pets.

Finally, this is not a book telling you where to find boondocking spots, but rather telling you how to find such spots and then maximize their use by setting up a comfortable, efficient, clean, and safe camp. I will give you tips on what to look for ahead of time. So, if you're wondering how you can live happily for free off-grid on your public lands, read on.

What is Boondocking?

Ask an RVer to define the term "boondocking," and you're likely to get a different answer from each person. Some consider it to be camping without hookups (water, sewer, and electricity), no matter where you're actually located, whether out in the woods or in a Walmart parking lot or even in an RV park with no hookups.

Some simply think of boondocking as "dry camping," which is essentially the same as camping with no hookups. Thus, to them, stopping for the night in a rest area by the highway or parking in a relative's driveway qualifies as boondocking.

But to many, boondocking is equated with what's called "dispersed camping," a term used by those who govern our public lands (such as the Bureau of Land Management, or BLM). For the purposes of this book, this is the definition I'll typically use.

Dispersed camping technically is camping outside of campgrounds on public lands (or private, with permission). Camping on public lands has its own rules and regulations that dictate where one can and can't camp and for how long (more on that later). Some also call this form of camping "free camping" and "wild camping," as such sites are typically off-grid out in nature. Another term is "primitive camping," though I've seen some boondocking rigs that can surpass a luxury apartment and are far from primitive.

Stealth Camping

Another form of camping is called "stealth camping" (also sometimes called "pirate camping") and is usually associated with camping in urban areas. A hard-core boondocker might sometimes engage in stealth camping while going from one boondocking area to another (called "turtling" by some).

Stealth camping is just as it sounds, camping in places where one might not be welcome, so therefore stealth is necessary. This would include some parking lots and city streets, and while doing so, one typically tries not to advertise that they're living in their vehicle. Those who want or need to stealth camp usually live in vans or box-type trucks, as it's hard to be stealthy in an RV.

An entire subculture revolves around stealth camping, with forums about necessities such as blackout curtains, disguising your rig to look like a work van or truck, dealing with the police, and other techniques for living under the radar. Many stealth campers have jobs in the area where they camp and simply don't want to (or can't) pay for a rental. Some live the RV lifestyle because they have pets or chemical sensitivities and can't find anyplace that will accommodate them.

For some, stealth camping is a statement about society—a refusal to conform—which also holds for some boondockers. Both types tend to be self-sufficient and frugal.

But the boondocker is typically different from the stealth camper in that they love the freedom and independence found in the natural world, and thereby seek out places far off-grid where they can be alone in the peace and quiet.

Stealth camping can be more of a permanent lifestyle, whereas boondocking may simply be for a vacation, though there also are plenty of full-time boondockers. Stealth campers need to keep a low profile, while boondockers typically don't, as what they're doing is perfectly legal. In any case, many techniques and methods apply to both.

Boondockers like seclusion and are willing to trade not having hookups for having privacy, although the more connected boondockers will have pretty much everything they could get in an RV park—communications (cell phone, internet), climate control (by using solar and propane), electricity (generated by solar), refrigeration and the ability to cook tasty nutritious foods, hot showers, and even movies. But some are happy with just a good book and a cup of coffee.

Any more, camping in a remote area doesn't mean you can't be in touch. Many great boondocking locations have good cell and internet coverage, sometimes even better than the RV parks.

In short, boondocking can be as primitive or civilized as you wish to make it. No matter what you call it, boondockers have one thing in common—they like to get away from it all.

Why Boondock?

There are many reasons for boondocking, but they generally fall into the following categories:

• Freedom: being able to do what you want when you want.

• It's fun: there's something about the simplicity of being outdoors away from it all that frees the mind, allowing you to be like a kid again and enjoy the simple things.

• Safety: in spite of what some may think, boondocking is far safer than any other type of camping. Because you're off the beaten path, the likelihood of anyone bothering you is very small, as you're probably the only camper for miles.

• No hassles with pets: you don't have to worry if an RV park or campground will accept your pets, plus you have greater freedom with them (can hike where you want, let them go off-leash if they stay close, and nobody complains if they bark).

• Save money: boondocking, by definition, is always free. You will have initial setup costs for the equipment you need, but after that, there's very little if any cost, except for your daily supplies and gas.

• Live in nature: there's nothing like watching a sunset with nothing or no one to impede your view, and wild animals, such as deer and birds, are much more likely to visit you in their own habitat. Most nature and wildlife photographers are avid boondockers.

• Experience life more fully: boondocking (and camping in general) allows you to learn about yourself, how you measure risk, and how you deal with living on the edge. Boondocking isn't necessarily risky or edgy, but it can be, and it will sometimes take you from your comfort zone, allowing you to become more confident and grow as a person.

• Solitude: boondockers can get into places where there's literally nobody around for miles and experience true peace and quiet. Seclusion is probably the main reason most people boondock, although economic reasons are becoming more and more prevalent.

• Explore new places: if you're set up to camp anywhere, you can take the road less-graveled and see where it goes. Being prepared to live off-grid means you're free to go where you want to go. And you don't need to go far if you don't want to, as there's usually something new to see nearby.

• Have few rules and regulations: as long as you follow the rules for the public land you're camped on, no one will bother you, and most of the rules for public lands are very simple.

• Nice campsites: along with no camping fees, you also can select your own campsite. Depending on where you go, this usually means beautiful scenery and a spacious and roomy campsite where you can set out your screen tent, chairs and table wherever you want.

• Change your front yard whenever you want: when boondocking, you have the freedom to live anywhere you want, whether in the mountains, the desert, by a lake, or next to a babbling creek. You can move as often as you wish. You can go to a place and stay as long as the rules allow, then move to another spot, exploring the countryside.

• Don't like the neighbors? Just move: you can easily change your neighborhood when you have the ability to live anywhere. All you have to do is turn the key. No more bad neighbors when boondocking—at least, not for long.

• Live in places even the wealthy can't afford: when boondocking, you can stay near national parks, reveling in scenery that even the rich can't buy. Or, you can stay in areas where only the wealthy can afford to actually live, yet without their housing expenses.

We'll examine the above factors in more detail in later chapters as well as explore other benefits to boondocking.

Things to Consider

If you've never camped before, boondocking will be a new experience, one that might leave you feeling out of your comfort zone, even if it's something you've always wanted to do. You'll be dealing with a wide range of emotions, as well as trying to figure out new equipment while making sure you have everything you need. And to make things even more interesting, everything can be more intense if you're alone.

This is why most first-time boondockers choose to take short excursions close to home, some even camping in their driveways for a few days. Trial runs can be educational, making the real thing go smoothly and without incident.

This is not meant to make boondocking sound difficult, it's simply that when one is going to be totally self-reliant, it's smart to check everything out before you're way out in the boonies, where you might have to cut your trip short if you forget something. It's always better to go prepared, although some things are learned mostly through experience. And if you're going full-time, it's even more important to make sure everything works, as you may not have a home to return to.

However, if you're a seasoned camper, you'll already have a good idea of things you'll need (a list of common items is provided later in this book). You'll also have previously dealt with first-time uncertainties and emotions that come with things that go bump in the dark (which are typically nothing to worry about). But it's still a good idea to have a test run, even if just one night in your driveway.

If you're thinking of going full-time and making boondocking a new way of life, it's best to do some research beforehand. Some people are confident enough to sell their houses and get rid of most of their possessions before even trying it out, but be aware that the average time on the road for full-timers is around two to three years, so plan accordingly.

You may not be average, but it's still best to have a backup plan. There's lots of information on the internet about people living the boondocking life—spend some time reading about what others are doing and see if it appeals to you.

Boondocking can take a different mindset than general RVing, as it allows one to be more spontaneous and free-spirited. There's a big difference between staying in RV parks and in camping wherever you find the next good spot. If you're a security-minded person, boondocking might not be for you, or at the very least, you might need to plan your boondocking spots ahead of time, which often is hard to do. Usually, you won't know where you'll be staying until you actually get there, and nothing can be reserved in advance. There will be times when you won't be able to find a spot you like and may spend the night in a parking lot.

If you're not a flexible person, you may find the uncertainties of boondocking very difficult. You can learn to be flexible, but it will require you to step out of your comfort zone, especially if you're used to a life of routine. Not everyone enjoys uncertainty, and some of us require more structure in our lives. This is another reason to do some test runs before committing to this as a lifestyle, and not liking it simply means you're of a different mindset, which is fine. But it's best to know before you invest a lot of money and time into a lifestyle you'll hate.

Be aware, however, that many so-called "boondockers" simply dry camp on graded roads, primarily because they have big rigs that can't go anywhere else. These big rigs typically have very little clearance, large generators, high wattage solar panels that require a big rig to carry them, satellite TV, big holding tanks, etc. You'll see literally thousands of such rigs at Quartzite, Arizona in the winter, spread all across the desert, "boondocking," but virtually unable to get anywhere that's not pretty much flat and smooth. They're off-grid, but not by far.

This is fine, there's nothing wrong with going that direction if you want, but be aware you'll never be able to actually get off-road where most of the good boondocking is. If you actually want to get away from it all, you'll need at the very least a high-clearance vehicle (we'll discuss the best rig to have later). Good boondocks on well-graded roads are rare, and if you find one, you can be guaranteed everyone else will probably also know about it.

Why Do You Want to Boondock?

It's important to ask yourself this question and then try to honestly answer it.

If you're trying to escape your current life, that's fine, and this is possibly the number one reason for people choosing this as a full-time lifestyle. But be aware that even though living in a new environment can often provide the change one needs, there is certain baggage you bring with you no matter where you go.

If you think that a change in environment will also result in you doing all the things you know you should be doing, especially those things that require self-discipline (like eating right and exercising), odds are good you'll soon fall back into your bad habits unless you make a real effort not to. Simply having a new lifestyle is not going to change you unless you really want to change, and you can change anywhere if you're determined enough.

Of course, having more opportunities to hike and exercise can make changing old habits easier, as will not having easy access to junk food. But any kind of change will still require motivation and discipline on your part.

If you're wanting to get away from a stressful life (and who wouldn't?), stop and ask yourself if you have the mindset to live off-grid, and if it's possible that you'll create new forms of stress in a new life. Some are good at creating stress no matter where they are, while others can relax once they're away from it all. But nothing is ever truly stress free, as some stress is just part of life. And boondocking can have its own set of stressors, things like worrying about incoming bad weather and safety. Sometimes you just trade one set of problems for another, as they say.

Are you looking for a cheaper way to live? When economic times are hard, more and more people look for creative ways to reduce their expenses. If you already own a rig, boondocking can be a cheap way to live, but if you're not happy living in the outdoors, saving money has less relevance. And you will still need an income, unless you're retired.

Is it cheaper to boondock than live in a dwelling? Well, it depends on whether you own your rig or have payments, as some vehicle payments can be more than a cheap apartment, but all things being equal, I know a number of boondockers who live on less than $1,000/month. They have no debt, are extremely frugal, and don't move their rigs until they have to so they're not spending money on gas. So, if you're looking at this lifestyle from the viewpoint of economic necessity, given that you have an income or means to make money on the road, it can be done for very little. But you'll want to have an emergency fund for equipment failures and such. Reread this last sentence, because if you break down on the road, it's much more critical than if you have a home, for your rig is your home. You need an emergency fund.

If you want to boondock because you love the simple things in life, it's a lifestyle that may really suit you. If you value freedom and are self-sufficient and flexible, then it may be a perfect way to live.

And if you're going off-grid because you have a sense of adventure, are independent and resourceful, and simply want to get out and enjoy nature away from everyone and lots of rules, boondocking is a great way to go.

Giving up Conveniences

Not all that long ago, boondocking meant giving up many of the conveniences of modern life, but this isn't as true now, especially in the technological sense.

You can get cell-phone coverage in many remote places, as well as the internet, which means you can watch movies on your tablet or other devices, as well as read and write blogs, post your photos, check the news and weather, and email friends and family. It's easier than ever to stay connected.

There are other things that you will have to do without or be resourceful, and your choice of a rig will help decide what they are. For example, if you're in a rig without much water storage, you're going to have to forego taking frequent showers, and even then, you'll learn to get clean with only a gallon or two of water.

Most rigs don't have much storage, so you'll also have to keep your needs simple, as well as try to not generate much trash. And eating fresh food will become a function of how often you can go to town and how large your refrigerator is, as well as how you generate the electricity to run it.

There will also be times when you have no choice but to rough it when it comes to temperatures, as your rig won't have the same ability to control the climate as a house would, being less insulated and having less effective appliances. When it's really cold out, your heater may not be able to keep up, making it necessary for you to get out more blankets. And unless you have a generator, running an AC is not an option. Most boondockers follow the seasons and become snowbirds to reduce these discomforts.

If you're used to being entertained, you'll have some adjusting to do while boondocking, as the only entertainment you'll have is generally what you yourself can provide. Of course, nature itself can be pretty entertaining (wildlife watching, storm tracking, etc.), but boondocking is not a life for those who are easily bored and don't have interests they can follow while camping. And you need to be comfortable with quiet and solitude.

How Self-Reliant Are You?

When out in the boonies, you can't just pick up the phone when your roof starts leaking in a storm or you smell propane. How good are you at dealing with such things? Can you change a tire or use a come-along to get unstuck? What would you do if your vehicle breaks down in the outback, especially knowing that most towing services either won't come that far out or will charge you a fortune if they do?

I recently read the blog of a fellow who had gone to Alaska in his big Class A RV (Class As are the big RVs that look like tour buses). On his way back down, he had a series of very bad luck breakdowns that ended up stranding him for weeks and costing thousands of dollars. It all started with a flat tire that he couldn't fix by himself while in the Yukon. After sitting by the road for several days (with no cell service), he finally found a mechanic who would come and repair his tire, but it cost him $1500 dollars, as they had to come from Tok, Alaska. He finally made it into the town of Whitehorse, where his tow vehicle broke down, costing more time and money, as parts had to be shipped from the U.S.

His case was somewhat extreme, and you may not find yourself quite as far in the outback, but do you have the ability and presence of mind to troubleshoot and repair your rig when you're out all alone, or at the very least, figure out how to get it done?

Not being mechanically inclined does not preclude you from boondocking, but it does make it more imperative to run a tight ship. You need to have your rig serviced frequently and take good care of your stuff, hopefully having things in good repair to start with. Recently, my alternator went out in a remote part of Idaho. The first (and only) vehicle to come by stopped and offered to help, but they didn't have jumper cables. Fortunately, I did and was able to utilize their help to get to the nearest town. It's important that you plan ahead for such things and have the proper equipment (more on this later). Of course, a lot of this applies with any kind of travel, but with boondocking, you are often in more remote areas.

One of the most important things a camper can have is the boondocker mindset, the ability to live with uncertainty and to even thrive on the unknown. Those who prefer to have everything pre-planned like a connect-the-dots picture usually don't do well with not having everything all planned out.

The happy boondocker is different in that they enjoy the adventure of not knowing exactly where they'll spend the next night, even if they have a general idea, and aren't upset when things don't work out as planned. They tend to roll with the punches and are quick to recover from setbacks. They're more interested in adventure and exploration than in safety and security. They like challenges.

Finally, don't let any of these considerations scare you off. These are simply things to be aware of—it's always good to know one's weaknesses. Probably the biggest deterrent to people trying out boondocking is fear of the unknown, but once they get out and try it, they realize how irrational most fears are, especially if one goes prepared. Most trips are uneventful and enjoyable.

What's the Best Rig for Boondocking?

Photographers have a saying that the best camera is the one you have with you when that great shot comes up. It's a similar thing with boondocking—the best rig is the one you have, though of course some rigs can certainly be improved on. And if you don't have a rig, the best one to buy for boondocking will always have tradeoffs.

I've seen people boondock in huge 40-foot Class As, and I've seen people camping in the wilds way off the grid in no more than a tent or in the back of their car. There are people who boondock in a Prius, whose batteries can serve to heat and/or cool the car while you sleep, providing a type of generator. I even know a man who uses his dirt bike to pull a small homemade trailer, though I'm not sure how legal it all is, though he made it to Baja for his first winter. Vans are also very popular.

Of course, the best rig is the one that will get you to where you want to go and then provide shelter and comfort while there. And the best rig is also the one you can buy for cash, freeing yourself from the burden of a monthly payment.

But if one could buy anything they wanted, what's the best rig for getting off the grid and out into the wilds? The answer to that question depends on you and your own likes and dislikes, as well as your own abilities and comfort levels.

For example, I once stopped at a rest area near Denali National Park in Alaska, where I saw an old beat-up RV pulling a similarly old beat-up pickup, the truck having the words "Alaska or Bust" painted on the side. An older couple was driving it, and I have to admit to thinking they must be pretty intrepid to have made it up there in that rig (they had Alabama plates). In the back of the pickup was a snow-mobile (snowmachine if you're in Alaska), so it looked like they were planning on staying for awhile.

I marveled at their hardiness, even though I myself was spending the summer tent camping, which probably in-volved a higher level of discomfort than their version. But to me, driving my SUV around and sleeping in a tent or even in the back was something quite manageable, while the thought of trying to maintain and buy gas for that old RV wasn't something I wanted to do.

So, we all have different comfort levels, and what's best for you might not be the same for me. I wouldn't know where to start to keep an old rig going, while you might be a master mechanic and have no problems with it.

I personally prefer to not pull a trailer, even though I've owned eight to date and have taken them all over the coun-try. I loved my trailer phase and experimented with many different types before deciding I preferred the simplicity of a tent and being able to just take off on some side road to see where it goes. Some folks pull large trailers and have no problems getting way out there, but their stress level has to be lower than mine. Not everyone prefers serendip-ity to comfort.

Another factor is whether or not you're going to be a full-timer or just go out for shorter trips. If you're living in a rig full time, you night want a higher level of comfort and security and more storage, whereas if you're just camping for a short time, you might not mind sacrificing some comfort for the ability to get further out into the backcountry.

The choice of rig also depends on how many of you there are. If you're going to travel alone, you can travel much lighter than if you bring your family along. Same with pets—the number will help dictate the size of your rig, though they typically don't require much space. And add to all this the degree to which you're willing to rough it.

But for me, as a single traveller with dogs and sometimes even a cat or two, the best boondocking vehicle would be something like the Tiger RV or a Sportsmobile, both which have the capability to get you out pretty much as far as the road will go, while also providing a comfortable living space, though limited size-wise. Many consider these the ultimate backroad vehicles, though there are some that are even more extreme, like the Earthroamer and the various Unimog-like vehicles. None are cheap, and some cost more than a nice house in some parts of the country.

Regardless of size or comfort level, there are a few things that all boondocking vehicles need:

1/ Four-wheel drive and good clearance. I admit that I rarely need my four-wheel drive, but it's nice to have a rig with that capacity. Clearance will let you get into places you maybe shouldn't go, and four-wheel drive will help you get back out.

You should at the very least be able to drive your vehicle over the equivalent of a street curb, at a minimum. The higher clearance your vehicle has, the more remote you can get. I do know boondockers without four-wheel drive who do just fine, but it will limit you somewhat.

2/ A way to power your rig, which is typically solar or a generator. I prefer solar, as it's quiet, clean, and doesn't need fuel. You'll want energy for the blower on your heater, your lights, refrigerator, computer, cell phone, and other electronics. Without an energy source, you'll quickly feel isolated and like you're living a third-world lifestyle, which you will be. I know people who use their vehicle to charge their smaller electronics (iPad, phone, etc.) and use solar lights and seem to do well, so once again, it depends on your levels of comfort, but even a small solar panel will make life much more enjoyable, and we're not talking a huge expense.

3/ The ability to carry enough food and water to stay out for awhile—the limit for most folks I know who boondock seems to be about two weeks before they want to get fresh food, dump their tanks and trash, and get a town fix. Food isn't hard to carry, but water can be, and you can live for a month without food, but only a few days without water. You should always be prepared for an emergency stay.

4/ The ability to have at least a moderate form of climate control. Be sure you have some form of heater. I've had more trips cancelled or made uncomfortable from a lack of heat than from anything else. Good insulation will help with both heating and cooling, but when it gets really cold, you need a heater, whether it be a forced-air propane heater built into your rig or a portable one, like the Little

Buddy. Having the ability to run an AC requires a generator, and there are many methods you can use to stay cool
(shade), but heat is important if you get cold. More people
die of hypothermia in the wilds than any other cause.

There are also things you're better off not having with
your rig, like a trailer made with rivets, slide-outs, and du-
ally wheels. More about these later.

The above are things most people consider necessary
for boondocking. Let's put these together to determine
what's the best rig for going off the beaten path.

What Size Should You Get?

Getting the right rig is probably the one thing that can
make or break your camping experience—too small can be
frustrating, as can too large, but what size you really need
can only be determined by you.

I've seen single people in large fifth-wheel trailers and
couples with kids and dogs in tiny trailers. Everyone has
their own levels of tolerance, and what you're willing to
give up is an individual choice. Some are minimalists and
don't want much, while others want all the comforts of
home.

Those in smaller rigs tend to view camping as an outdoors experience, and they compensate for the small space
by making the outdoors part of their habitat. These are the
same people who would live in a small house or apartment
if not on the road, for they really don't need much. They
value experience over possessions.

Of course, this is a generalization, and those who are
on the road for financial reasons might prefer a nice big

house. But generally, I've found that those who have smaller rigs tend to be minimalists. They don't want to spend their time tending to their big Class A motorhome, nor do they want to be restricted in where they can camp because of size.

Standard stick-built trailers (non-molded fiberglass) are usually a foot wider than the molded-fiberglass trailers (think Casita or Scamp or Escape), which gives you more room, but also makes them a bit harder to handle. And if you get a small rig, big windows can make a world of difference (but you will need good insulating curtains).

I have seen some huge rigs out in the boondocks (particularly at Quartzite), but not in places that are difficult to get into. Those with the big rigs tend to value comfort more than flexibility and don't mind paying to feed these gas hogs, as well as the extra costs for maintenance and upkeep. They enjoy having lots of interior space. Some of these rigs are downright luxurious.

If you're new to all this, the best advice you'll hear is to go small. First, your initial costs will be much lower, and if you decide you don't like the lifestyle, it's easier to recoup your investment, as smaller rigs are easier to sell and don't depreciate as much, generally, as there's more of a demand for them.

If you're boondocking, you're probably an outdoors-type person and will be outside a lot, so why get a big rig? You only need a place to sit and sleep, and the rest is just something you have to haul around. You may not be in it all that much unless the weather's bad.

It's common to see shade shelters, screen tents, and even large free-standing tents set up in a camp, as these can extend your living space and make things much more comfortable.

One or two people can live comfortably in a truck camper if they're not in it a lot (and they get along well). A small trailer (17 or 19 feet) is also big enough, but a 22 to 24 footer can feel downright luxurious. The main problem with going really small is storage space. I've seen people living full time in small teardrop trailers, and some even had pets, but they don't spend much time inside or carry much.

The bigger the rig, the more resources you're going to need to operate and move it, plus typically the more it will cost to buy. It will take more energy and a bigger tow vehicle to pull it around, as well as to heat and cool it. You'll spend more time and money fixing things, as the more systems a rig has, the more things that can break. And the bigger the rig, the fewer places you can take it.

And if you think you need a big rig for your stuff, be aware that much of the stuff you thought you needed will be rarely used. Most people tend to get rid of a lot of stuff after a few months on the road.

So, it's better to start with a smaller rig, assuming you really do want to boondock. If you're happy in campgrounds and RV parks, you may want more space. But you also don't want to go too small if there are more than one of you or you have several pets.

One of my first trailers was a little 13-foot fiberglass Burro, which is a molded-fiberglass trailer like a small Scamp. Even though I spent most of my time outside and loved the ease of pulling it, I finally traded up for a bigger one. I found there just wasn't enough space for me and three dogs and enough stuff to be able to stay out for more than a few days.

One thing to consider, especially if you're going to become a hard-core boondocker going into remote places on rugged roads, is whether or not your rig has rivets. Airstreams are highly-regarded (even though overly expensive), but are riveted, making them prone to having rivets pop out when subjected to bad roads. Casitas are the same, as are Scamps and some other molded-fiberglass trailers. Replacing rivets may not be on your bucket list. You may go for years without having any rivets pop out, then have a number go all at once.

If you have a truck/van and trailer combo, you'll find you have much more room to haul supplies, as the truck bed or van interior can act like a small storage unit. This makes pulling a small trailer much more manageable.

Once again, there's a big difference between boondocking for a vacation or even a summer and doing it full time. Living in a rig means you may want something bigger. You can also add roof carriers and bicycle racks for more space.

It can be tricky to get a rig that's big enough and yet can be taken into the backcountry.

New or Used?

This one's easy—always buy used, and preferably not from a dealer.

Some people think a dealer's the only place to buy, as a dealer will stand behind their product. This is sometimes the case, but more often, not. A dealer is a middleman between you and the manufacturer, and typically a dealer will refer you to the manufacturer for repairs, even for a new rig. Some dealers will fix defects if they have the shop and the manufacturer warrants it, but be prepared to wait, sometimes a long time, as in months. There are lots of horror stories out there, so do your research. Check out the dealer and manufacturer, as well as the model trailer or rig you're interested in. Dealers make the majority of their money from sales, not repairs, and many act accordingly.

And if you buy used from a dealer, typically it's "as is." RV dealers have gained a reputation that makes used car dealers look honest, so be informed. This isn't necessarily true of all dealers, of course, and a good one is worth their weight in gold, but most RV salespeople know less about what they sell than you do after a few hours of research on the internet.

Ironically, many people don't want to buy from private sellers because they worry they'll get ripped off. The opposite is generally true. And if you buy from a private person, you can always get a mechanic to check out the rig before buying.

As with all things, it's best to buy with cash. Dealers make buying easy, as they can help you get financing, and banks are more likely to give you a loan when you buy from a dealer. But you're also typically paying much more than you would from a private buyer, especially with the add-on fees most dealers don't tell you about until you're closing the deal.

If you do buy from a dealer, never pay asking price. Get on the internet and research what others have paid for similar rigs. A new rig can usually be had for up to 25% less than sticker, especially if you buy in the fall or winter when things are slow.

Another thing to be careful of when at a dealer's is not
to get hooked into buying options you don't need, options
that cost more, can break, and make your rig that much
heavier.

Keep in mind that a new RV will lose up to 40% of its
value in just a few years, which is another reason to buy
used. If you're making payments, after a short time, your
trailer will be worth less than what you owe.

On top of that, a new trailer typically has plenty of bugs
(unless you're buying a molded fiberglass trailer, which
are considered to be the best for durability). When you
buy used, many of the things that failed in the first couple
of years have been fixed. And many use their RVs only for
a few weeks a year, so a used rig can be like new without
paying a high price.

Also, if you're going to boondock, which usually means
going into remote spots, you're going to be on rough roads,
sometimes with your rig getting "pinstripes" from bushes
and trees. If you have a new rig, you're going to be less
inclined to want to get into these places, which are usually
the nicest spots.

If you're new to all this, another good reason to buy
used is that you may change your mind and decide you
don't like the lifestyle or that particular rig. You'll have less
of an investment in a used rig and thereby will take less of
a loss, if any, should you decide to sell. You'll simply have
less money tied up in a used rig.

Finally, most of us can't afford to buy new. In fact, a lot
of people can't really even afford to buy much of anything,
given today's economic climate. If you fall in this category, I
suggest you consider van-dwelling, which combines living

and sleeping quarters. Vans can be had fairly inexpensively compared to other RVs, are easy to setup for boondocking, and are probably the best rig for stealth camping. It may be harder to find a van with good clearance, but don't let that deter you, as there are many good boondocking spots that will still be accessible.

Four-Wheel Drive

The option of whether or not to have four-wheel drive depends in good part on whether or not you decide to pull a trailer. As mentioned above, vans typically are not four-wheel-drive, nor are Class A's, B's, or C's, though one can sometimes find conversions. Thus, you don't typically get the choice of four-wheel drive when you select one of these type of rigs.

What's a conversion? Well, for a fairly steep price (generally starting in the $10,000 range and up), you can take your rig to a company that specializes in turning it into a four-wheel drive vehicle. Sportsmobile is probably the most recognized of these, and they can also convert your rig into a complete RV, which is even more expensive. Quigley is another well-known company. Other shops can do this type of conversion, and I suspect that many are cheaper. Some people even do it themselves, but you need a shop, the knowledge, and tools.

You don't really need four-wheel drive to boondock, and many hard-core boondockers just have front-wheel drive. If you're careful about where you go, you can get away with not having it. Most national forest and state/national parks have well-maintained roads that a two-wheel drive vehicle won't have any trouble navigating. But having four-wheel drive is nice for one's peace of mind, knowing you can probably get unstuck if you do manage to get into a pickle.

But be aware that having four-wheel drive can also get you really stuck, as it may make you more confident than you should be and thereby result in you going places you really shouldn't. Getting a tow truck back into some places is either impossible or very expensive.

Assuming you decide to go with a trailer and tow vehicle, it's always good to get the best tow vehicle you can afford and put as little as you can get away with into the trailer part of the combo. It's expensive and often difficult to find a good tow vehicle, and trailers are easy to find. It's much easier to upgrade to a different trailer than to a different tow vehicle.

You don't have to buy a pickup to tow a trailer, as many vans are well-suited to the task, as are many SUVs, depending on the trailer's weight. Be sure to check the tow rating of the vehicle, and should you decide to ignore the manufacturer's advice about how much is safe for that vehicle to tow, be aware that you're setting yourself up for a ticket and/or lawsuit should you ever get in an accident, even if it's not your fault. And don't forget that the weight ratings can include you and whatever else you have in the vehicle, not just the weight of the trailer and the stuff you have in it (including in the tanks).

If you decide to use a pickup, having a topper will give you much more storage and security, as you can lock up your gear. This is one of the main complaints against fifth-wheel trailers—the hitch takes up the bed of the truck. Having a club cab can also be helpful for locking things up, as well as having your pets ride with you for heat and warmth and their security. (Never let your pets ride in your trailer.)

A V8 engine will provide you with plenty of power for headwinds and mountains. Yes, you'll lose some money in gas mileage, but if you're full-timing, you'll soon find that you can take it slow and easy. There's no hurry to get anywhere and you also won't be on the road as much as if you were just on vacation. I know boondockers who never leave the state of Arizona, as one can be quite comfortable in the desert there in the winter and the Arizona mountains in the summer. Many boondockers put fewer miles on their rigs than they did while working a regular job.

And as for dualies (dual wheels on the rear axle of your truck or rig), many boondockers don't like them as rocks can get stuck between the dual tires and damage the sidewalls, as well as get thrown against the underside of the truck. Don't confuse dualies with dual axles, which usually provide more stability and are found on heavier trailers.

Clearance

Clearance can be a real issue (or rather, lack of it) when boondocking. Even though one can get away without having four-wheel drive, good clearance is a real necessity.

How much clearance does one generally need? As mentioned before, if you can easily drive up and over a curb, you're probably going to be fine most if the time, though there will be occasions when you'll be stopped by a bumpy road or a wash.

You can sometimes order a trailer with a high-lift axle, which will give you a few inches of extra ground clearance.

Better still, buy used and have a shop install this for you or do it yourself. Leaf springs mounted over the axle can also be helpful.

Some trailers come in an off-road model, like some hardside popups like the Aliner Expedition and the Chalet Explorer. Such trailers will have a lifted axle and larger tires, both contributing to more clearance. A four-wheel drive pickup will usually have all the clearance you'll need and exceed that of whatever trailer you might pull.

Sometimes the limiting factor in getting into a site isn't clearance, but is length. If you decide to buy a long trailer, expect to be shut down by twisty roads and sharp curves, sometimes in places where it's almost impossible to back down the way you came. Fifth-wheel trailers are two or three feet taller than regular trailers and are also usually lengthy, so fewer people choose to boondock with these.

There will also be times when your overhead clearance isn't going to get you through all those forest branches (one reason some don't like pickup campers, as they have a high profile, unless you get a popup). I've seen people get on top of their rigs and cut branches off, but this is probably frowned upon by those whose job it is to patrol the forest (and who often have the authority to write tickets).

And though this isn't really about clearance, it's also helpful to have a rig that won't rock too much when on tippy roads (which some pickup campers will do, testing the limits of their camper tie-downs). If your rig has a separate body from the cab, bad roads can be damaging to the vehicle as the vehicle twists and rocks. Pickup beds can be examples of this, and adding a big heavy camper can set you up for potential damage. Vans are examples of a full-body vehicle and aren't as prone to this.

In addition, some rigs have very poor visibility when going up over a steep area, and there's nothing more disconcerting to be climbing a steep hill and not being able to see anything but your hood.

And finally, slide-outs are very prone to failure when subjected to the tough roads of the boondocker. The constant motion can be very hard on the seals, as well as the slide mechanisms, and if you can't get your slide-out back in, you're pretty much stuck in place. Not something you want out in the middle of the boonies, for sure.

Heating and Cooling

Whether you have a heater built into your rig or carry a portable one, I consider one a necessity. I carry a Little Buddy heater when I tent camp, which has many times made my trip much more comfortable.

Spending most of my time in Colorado, Utah, Montana, and the North (Canada and Alaska), I would never buy a rig without a heater. Good insulation also goes a long ways towards comfort in both the cold and heat.

Solar is the preferable way to go, in my opinion. It's quiet and will usually generate power even on a cloudy day. If you have enough wattage (120 to 200 watts is usually more than enough), you can also run things like your refrigerator and a crockpot, though air conditioning is pretty much impossible, as it takes too much power (typically around 800 watts).

AC is not necessary unless you decide to stay in hot places in the summer. The beauty of boondocking is that you can follow the seasons, so most full-timers go where it's warm in the winter and cool in the summer. I've found that generators are not popular items when camping around others, and I prefer to not deal with the expense, noise, maintenance, and having to carry gas. Solar is much easier and doesn't disturb the peace.

There are things one can do to help keep your rig warm or cool, such as insulating the windows with Reflectex or heavy curtains and putting rugs on the floor. When it's hot or raining, having an awning is a real plus. If your rig didn't come with one, you can have one installed or do it yourself. Be sure it's manual so you don't end up using power you need for other things. An awning will keep your rig cool inside as well as provide outside shade and rain protection.

It's best to keep an eye out for winds if you have your awning out, and I always roll mine up if I'm going to be gone. It's also a good idea to put a bungee cord around it before traveling so the wind can't catch it and pull it off.

Insulation

We tend to think of insulation as being something we want when it's cold, but insulation can also serve to keep you cool as well as to deaden outside noise. Though you generally won't have much noise when boondocking, it can be major when you're in campgrounds or turtling in Camp Walmart.

And even if you don't intend to camp anyplace that's cold, you'll still want backup warmth, as even places like Arizona and Florida can get cold, as illustrated by the 2015 El Nino where parts of southern Arizona got snow and frost.

If you do intend to full-time and be in your rig year-round, or to just be able to boondock in comfort whenever you want, look for a four-season unit, whether a trailer, pickup camper, or motorhome (Born Free and Bigfoot both can be bought with four-season insulation). Four-season units typically cost more, but are worth it if you can swing it. One of their main advantages is thermal windows and heated holding tanks, but there are a number of things you can do if your rig doesn't have these, such as thermal curtains and cutting insulating materials (Reflectix) to fit into each window at night.

Which brings us to window sizes. As mentioned above, a smaller trailer will feel much larger if it has large windows, but these can also be a liability if it's cold. It will be important for you to doctor them up with removable insulating materials for cold weather. And if it's raining, some windows must be closed to prevent water from leaking inside, which can make it hot and muggy in the rig. Rain gutters can alleviate this problem, allowing you to keep your windows open, and jalousie windows can be left open without getting things inside wet. (Jalousie windows are the kind that have several horizontal panels that crank open.)

Slide-outs are typically not very well insulated in order to keep them lightweight so they can easily slide in and out, another good reason to not have them.

It seems that the northern manufacturers (Bigfoot, Escape, and Northwoods, maker of Arctic Fox and Nash) are the place to go for four-season trailers and campers, and all of these three manufacturers have good reputations. There are others that I'm not as familiar with that may be just as good or better. It pays to do your research.

The Ideal Rig

For me personally, the ideal rig is the pickup-camper combo. It has its pluses and minuses, but it's the easiest of all vehicles to get off the beaten path while its shorter length also allows you to park in regular parking spaces when in town, places most RVs can't fit. You can easily stealth camp in them, and they have the capacity to hold enough food and water for lengthy stays. It's easy to just pull off the road and camp about anywhere for the night, which makes road trips much less stressful.

A pop-up truck camper has a low profile for going into tricky places (under trees) and is also very cost-effective for gas mileage. Truck campers can be very expensive (think Bigfoot or Lance or Arctic Fox), but the popups can be bought used for only a few thousand dollars.

All in all, this is the ideal rig for me, but if there is more than one on the trip, it can get crowded. In my experience, smaller rigs like this make camping, exploring, and finding solitude much easier. But once again, we're each unique in what we need to make our travels better.

In conclusion, the type of rig you need will depend on factors such as how many will be along for the ride (size) and for how long (storage), as well as the seasons you intend to camp (insulation, heating and cooling). Where you wish to camp is also a consideration, as this will determine how large and capable (clearance, four-wheel drive) your rig needs to be. And of course how much you wish to spend, both initially and in repairs and future gas monies, will also be important.

Being Independent

If you're a boondocker, you have to be fairly independent. You have to know how to take care of yourself as well as have the means to contact someone to help you with things you can't do. Those are pretty much your two choices, especially if you travel solo.

I've found that if you set emergency procedures in place before going out you'll have a much better experience and be less nervous about what to do if something happens. Also, having a weather radio will help you be prepared for whatever's coming weather wise (more on this later).

Most people who are serious RVers have roadside assistance, whether it be as a rider on their own vehicle insurance, such as with Geico, or through companies such as Good Sam, who will sell you a separate insurance that will cover your RV and its contents, as well as come out and change flat tires and provide other roadside assistance (theoretically, though most won't assist you if you're off the road very far).

Some companies also have medical assistance programs that will transport you back home if you are unable to drive, take your vehicle back home for you, and even take care of your pets and make sure they get back home.

Be sure to read the fine print on such policies, for even though they may provide assistance, some will charge you extra for some things. For example, the Good Sam medical assistance program will charge you extra for returning your pets to your home and making sure they're okay. But, in this case, you're probably happy to just know someone's doing it and would gladly pay an extra price.

Be aware that most policies will not cover roadside assistance if you're not on a recognized road such as a county road, and some even stipulate that the road must be paved. Such policies will do you no good if you're boondocking in the backcountry and have problems.

Some people who are not handy will not boondock for fear of breaking down and not being able to get out. However, if you have a cell phone, most areas are covered, and if you have the means and are a serious backcountry camper, you can always buy or rent a satellite phone.

The most important consideration in boondocking is to keep your equipment in good repair. If you are not confident about your mechanical abilities, making sure everything is shipshape can allay the majority of your fears. For example, keep your tires aired up, keep your battery in good shape, and always have a voltmeter with you for troubleshooting, assuming you know how to fix things.

You can also carry equipment that will help you in minor emergencies, such as a portable air compressor or canned air in case you have a flat tire, or such things as tire plugs. But these things won't do you any good if you don't know how to use them.

So, it's best to keep your vehicle in good condition and understand the basics of maintenance and repair. It helps to be handy and have a good dose of common sense, but there are a lot of elderly people who boondock and wouldn't be able to fix anything major, but they don't let that stop them.

One nice thing about boondocking is that usually someone else will eventually come along and help you out if you have a problem, but it's best not to count on this and to be prepared.

One handy item that everyone should carry is a personal locator beacon, also called a PLB. This is a device that can be activated in case of emergency and will send a signal to a satellite that will then forward the emergency signal to local search and rescue. However, since rescues can be hours in the making, this is not necessarily a quick instant rescue, but PLBs have helped save many lives, and I highly recommend one. You can purchase them online (REI, Amazon) for a couple of hundred dollars. They have also saved the lives of those who don't carry them by being in the hands of someone who does and who came upon an emergency.

Having a medical condition should not necessarily stop you from boondocking, as long as you are careful and plan ahead. Many people who boondock take medications such as insulin or heart medicine. I'm always amazed at the number of people who camp with COPD and other chronic lung problems and use a CPAP machine in their rigs.

The same goes for your pets—they can have medical issues, and usually that shouldn't stop you from taking them camping with you, depending on the condition, of course. I camped for years with a dog that had diabetes and had to have an insulin shot twice a day. There may be times when you'll need to take your dog to the vet, but this will be similar to if you were at home, not much different, you just need to find a good vet wherever you are. I cover most of these issues in my book, RVing with Pets.

But the main difference between camping out in the boonies and living in a house is that you can't just run and grab something from your house or jump into your car and run into town (although sometimes you can, depending on how far out you're camped). So, it's important when camping in the outback that you anticipate possible emergencies and keep the necessary supplies. For example, you will want to have a first aid kit if you boondock with animals, as well as one for yourself.

What it boils down to is that you need to be self sufficient. This involves a certain level of common sense, as well as awareness. If you're forgetful, it's important that you use checklists to substitute for your memory. The last place you want to be without something important is in the back country.

Fortunately, there really isn't that much that you have to remember, just the basics for survival such as food and water, first aid kits, cell phone, and weather radio. Once you have these, you're set.

A lot of people will have a check list for when they break camp, which will include things like making sure your awning is rolled up tight, your levelers are up, the gas is turned off, and that sort of thing. I have a friend who's run over the portable step for his trailer so many times he's using baling wire to keep it together.

There really aren't any big secrets to successful boondocking. Most of it is common sense, and if you're not confident, you can always go out for short stays, gradually building up your confidence levels until you go out for as long as you want or even full-time.

Remember, most boondocking skills are not taught, but are learned in the school of experience. If you're really intimidated by it all, start out with friends, camping together until you're more confident. But most things are just learned by doing.

For example, it can be rather intimidating the first time you have to take your propane bottles off the trailer so you can take them into town to refill them. But after you've done it once, you realize it's really no big deal. You just turn them off, unscrew the connector, and lift them off.

The more you camp, the more experience you have, and the more you can predict future outcomes. For example, if you're camping where it's 40° at night, you'll soon realize that you can go a couple of weeks before you have to refill your two 20-pound propane bottles. Things quickly become second nature and you wonder why it seemed like such a big deal in the first place.

After a while, you get pretty good at coordinating everything, knowing when you need to refill propane bottles, water tanks, and dump your gray and black tanks, if you have them. This requires a trip into town, and you can plan ahead, knowing approximately when you'll need to restock and do all these things.

The real limiting factor again of course is water. It doesn't matter how much food or propane you have, if you run out of water, you have to go to town. As a rule of thumb, I generally use about three gallons a day for me and three dogs. That does not include any extra use such as doing dishes, taking showers, or that kind of thing, just drinking water.

It seems like a lot of boondockers work on a two-week cycle, going into town every couple of weeks to resupply, eat out, do laundry, etc. This also seems to be the general time period that people can go without socializing.

And this is usually when most people will also move camp, partly because of the need to resupply, but partly because two weeks is the general limit of staying at one spot on public lands.

Moving camp can be a lot of work—you have to hook up your trailer (if you have one) and pick up all your gear, such as your table, chairs, outdoor rug, water jugs, etc. It also costs money for the gas to move camp, which can be a limiting factor if you're on a tight budget.

It seems that people who travel light tend to move more often and also more freely, people such as those who live in vans or pickup campers. So, if you're the type of person who likes to travel a lot, it may be best to select a rig that's conducive to such. There's always a trade-off, and you'll be trading comfort for portability, but there's nothing more tiring then having to pick up a large camp.

For me, the real downside to boondocking is not bad weather, insecurity, or discomfort, it's having to haul a bunch of junk around. Those who are seasoned campers are often the ones with the least stuff.

Be careful what you start out with, as it's easy to create traditions you may not want later. For example, when starting out, it's easy to be in a rush and just throw things in, thinking that you'll organize everything when you get out to your camp spot. Unfortunately, the human memory is such that, even if it's not where you ultimately want it, you'll search for an object in the first place you happened to have put it.

Some people are real sticklers for organization and are better than others about keeping things in their place. This makes it easier to find stuff, but it does take a little extra effort when putting things away.

There's really no right or wrong way to boondock, and the main thing is to be prepared and be self-sufficient. Other than that, everyone has their own style, all the way from being chronically disorganized, as I tend to be, to being the kind of camper that you look in their trailer and feel like you're looking into a picture of Martha Stewart perfection.

I actually have a friend whose trailer is always immaculate, from the watercolor paintings on the wall to her handmade quilt, all in their place, no matter the weather or location. Then I know another who has to be careful when he opens his door, as something may fall out. I tend to be somewhere in the middle, depending on the day and weather and other unknown factors.

Boondocking is a work of art, independence, and self-sufficiency, and, just like the rest of the human race, no two boondockers are the same, nor are their styles. The main question is, are you having a good time? That's the true standard of measurement. Do things your way, just be prepared.

Dealing with Boredom and Loneliness

Probably the most difficult thing for the solo camper is getting bored and/or lonely. Some people naturally have more of a loner mindset than others, but most everyone needs human company after awhile, even if it's just to go into town and look around, remembering that other humans exist.

We all need to be able to take care of ourselves to a certain degree, and this has an emotional component, a fact many forget until they're way out there and lonely and/ or feeling unsettled and maybe even a bit afraid. (I'll talk more about security and being safe later.)

There are things you can do to make yourself feel better, such as having a good radio to break the silence when you can't or don't want to go to town and get a people fix.

I've noticed that most full-time boondockers are eager to talk when they run into someone else in the outback, and it's surprising the number of friendships one can make when out in the middle of nowhere—probably because you have a lot in common and both need to talk.

Life on the road less graveled is definitely not something that everyone enjoys. Some people boondock just for a few days—sometimes just for variety, and sometimes because they're on the road to somewhere else—then go to a campground.

But the serious boondocker is a somewhat unique breed of person. The serious boondocker is typically a full-timer and never stays in campgrounds, though some will occasionally use a campground as a place to regroup and take a shower, get rid of trash, etc.

Some boondockers often will out-stay their two-week limit on public lands. They get deep into the backcountry and tend to stay in one spot, hoping they're never routed out by a ranger, and often they're not, depending on where they are and how many rangers patrol the area. This is a whole different ballgame, and it's somewhat akin to being a squatter. Often people who do this are boondocking from necessity, and don't have the funds to move from one place to another. Some like to live this way because they're introverted and enjoy solitude, and don't really care if they see new territory or not, but instead just enjoy the security and ease of staying in one place.

I've always found it somewhat ironic that boondockers will leave town to recover from civilization way out in the back country, and then occasionally return to town to recover from solitude, usually because they get lonely.

There are times when anyone who camps gets tired of their own internal monologue and wants human company. As humans, we're a pretty gimpy species and have always needed to be in groups to survive until only more recent times. We're genetically predisposed to want to be around other humans, even those of us who enjoy solitude. Even though we sometimes act like we think we are, we're not true apex predators, which are typically alone except to breed and raise their young. And we're not as capable of protecting ourselves when alone as an apex predator. For example, if you go hiking in grizzly bear country, the bear biologists will tell you to hike in groups of at least three for protection and carry bear spray.

We are herd animals, and we know there's safety in numbers. The solitary person who camps and hikes on his or her own is definitely not the norm. Like some species, only about typically two to three percent of us are genetically predisposed to wander and explore, thus ensuring the species is spread into as many regions as possible, thereby increasing the odds of survival of the species.

For example, almost all spawning salmon return to their birthplace, an amazing fact that biologists have determined is the result of chemical brain mapping. However, two to three percent of all salmon don't return home and instead go up new waterways to spawn.

But even the most independent person, and independence does seem to be a defining characteristic of most boondockers, needs an occasional people fix, or at the very least to drive around town and remember that there are other people on the planet, even if it's just so they can go back out and remember why they like being alone.

Some need to actually talk to others and will spend a few days in town, while others only need to regroup and are then happy to escape. Not all of us can eat Ramen noodles all of the time, and going into town helps us not only resupply, but to keep our lives in perspective.

Sometimes groups of people who like to boondock will hang together and travel separately but meet up down the road in a new spot. This provides companionship, security, and a different level of interest for some people. Others prefer solitude and almost never camp with anyone else.

Boondockers who camp together have to respect each other's boundaries or it doesn't work. Some people don't want to see another human being from their camp spot, while others don't mind as long as you're not too close.

They all tend to develop little rituals, if you want to call them that, or maybe schedules would be a better way to put it, where they do things together, such as walk the dogs in the morning at a certain time, or have dinner together at a certain time, that sort of thing. This provides people with a feeling of belonging, the security of knowing that if something goes wrong you have others there to help out, and just gives a general feeling of well-being.

If you want to boondock, but aren't as solitary as some, you can seek out these groups and they will generally welcome you. Most of them have at least one member that blogs on the internet, and you can start following RV blogs and eventually find someone in the area you want to be in that belongs to a small group.

In general, these groups tend to follow the weather like snowbirds, going south to Arizona in the winter, and further north in the summer. Some groups only gather together in the winter, and then will each go their own way for the summer, regrouping again the next winter.

Group members tend to come and go, and you may meet a different person or group that you prefer to boon-dock with, but the general result is that you're not isolated. There is a lot to be said for this, the security of knowing you have someone who can help you if you get stuck or sick or any number of things, but be aware that group dynamics do develop and like with any other human activity these can be either good or bad.

It's been my experience that those who are more introverted and enjoy solitude tend to do much better alone than in a group. Some people will initially join a group until they get their land legs and become more adept at camping, and then will wander off and spend more time alone than with others. We each have to follow our own native tendencies to be happy.

But back to loneliness. Being an introvert really helps, as you're good at entertaining yourself and doing things alone. Having a pet or two also helps. I know that I personally enjoy solitude, but if I do get lonely, it tends to be in the evenings when the sun is setting and darkness is moving in.

I've often wondered if this isn't a genetic predisposition harkening back to the times when we were hunter-gatherers and our only defense was to live in groups, and we knew that if we were caught alone out in the darkness we were at a huge survival disadvantage. We are not night animals and have poor night vision, so we need security at night. That's the only explanation I've been able to come up with for feeling lonely during that transition in the evening between day and night. I have also noticed that I don't feel this when I'm staying in a house, even if there are no other people around.

I have talked to other boondockers who say they feel the same thing. If they get lonely at all, it will typically be in the evening, and once they survive that, when night comes they're fine.

My own solution for this is to get busy and do something, even if it's just to read a book for an hour or two. If I am planning on moving camp, this is often a good time for me to do it as long as I know where I'm going so I'm not stumbling around in the dark.

And I will add that the evenings are always the time that I feel wanderlust the worst, wanting to hit the road and go somewhere new. Sometimes, if I'm not hooked up to a trailer, I'll just go for a short drive down the road.

This brings us to the topic of boredom. There really are only so many things you can do out in the back country, and it's easy to get tired of doing the same old things. The same patterns you have while living in a house are going to be the same patterns you have while boondocking, though you may express them differently.

For example, when I'm living in a house, I like to get up in the morning and have a cup of coffee, maybe check my emails and that sort of thing for a half-hour, then I'll get in the shower, get dressed, and get out and do something.

If I'm boondocking, I tend to follow the same patterns, except getting out to do something is much easier because I can typically just go for a hike from my front door.

If you're not sure if you're boondocking material, just take note of your daily patterns and then try to transpose them mentally onto what you would do if you were out in the backcountry.

We all need a certain level of structure, and it's been my experience that those who give up boondocking or camping in general tend to be people who find they miss that psychological security of routine. You can re-create this no matter where you are, but sometimes you have to be inventive.

Of course, some people give boondocking up because they find they don't like living without certain creature comforts. It's better to know thyself before you make the plunge and possibly sell your house and invest in a trailer rather than doing all that and finding out later you don't like it.

But if you're a person who likes routine, you need to develop routines that make you happy, even when you're out in the back country. In fact, routines may be more important out in the back country, as they provide you with a sense of security and control and ensure you're doing the things necessary for a good experience.

And so, the more you boondock, the more you tend to develop little routines. You get up in the morning, maybe step outside and watch the sunrise, feed the dogs, make a cup of coffee, and if you're set up for the internet you may check the weather, news, and your emails.

As an aside, most people who boondock seem happier if they have the internet, as it gives them a sense of being in touch with the outside world, as well as providing essential weather information and being able to contact other people and see what's going on.

You can check out new boondock sites with Google Earth or by reading other boondockers' blogs, and that sort of information does make your life easier in general. Being on the internet can reduce not just loneliness but also your levels of boredom, and this goes for anywhere, though it's harder to be an internet addict when boondocking because of energy constraints, though I have met a few.

I've found that if I am getting bored, it's usually time to move camp. Finding a new camp spot makes things interesting again, as there are new places to explore, photograph, etc.

But what do people do for entertainment when boondocking, especially if they're alone? Well, it just depends on what you like to do. Some people like to read, others like to write, some do photography, some enjoy hiking a lot, some people like to play solitary games, some people do martial arts, some do watercolors—the list is endless.

You can do just about anything you would do at home, unless your hobby requires a lot of materials, such as quilting. (I do know a woman who makes quilts while boondocking, but she lives in a large trailer.)

One thing I like about the internet is that it gives you the ability to plan your next move, and you can spend a lot of time doing that, which may include checking out new places to explore, locations of things you may want to visit (the library, historical sites, gourmet restaurants, etc.).

Finding and exploring new places is part of the fun of boondocking. You can spend quite a few hours doing this, and I've found that if I get bored, this can be a fun way to decrease my boredom.

But essentially, the cure for boredom and loneliness is within you. If you take up boondocking thinking you'll be totally happy just admiring the scenery and hiking, this may be true for a time, but you will eventually get bored.

You can do many of the same things you enjoy doing at home, and even if you find a nice spot and want to stay there for some time, keep in mind that part of the destination is the journey, as they say, and as a free spirit, you need to exercise that freedom and see new places in order to be really happy.

So, what do people do while camping?

Photography is a great hobby. It's a lot of fun, and you don't really need much equipment, just a camera and maybe a lens or two, and you can download your photos directly onto your computer.

A lot of boondockers have laptops that are easily re-charged from solar—if you have a pure sinewave inverter, you can charge any kind of electronic equipment, even the very sensitive stuff.

Another popular hobby is geocaching. You can look for other peoples' caches, as well as create your own. The website geocaching.com seems to be the central hub for all this, and some people travel all over the country looking for geocaches and attending geocache events.

Some people enjoy art, especially landscape painting. Plein air painting is very popular with the boondocking crowd, for obvious reasons.

A lot of craft-based hobbies are space intensive, in that they require a lot of materials and can be overwhelming in a small trailer or RV. But things like needlepoint can be easily done, satisfying the creative urge.

A nice compact hobby is HAM radio, which seems to be popular with many boondockers. HAM radio also serves as an important communications tool. Sadly, this hobby seems to be dying out, probably because it's so easy to communicate with cell phones any more.

Probably one of the more popular RV hobbies is blog-ging. Some bloggers have a lot of followers who leave interesting and informative comments. Many bloggers meet up at bloggerfests, and a lot of friendships have been formed this way.

Some people are into radio-controlled airplanes and drones and will take them into the backcountry. Drones are becoming more and more regulated as more and more people buy them and are now illegal in national parks, primarily because of the noise and the effect they have on wildlife. RC airplanes and drones are probably better in more urban areas where they have their own dedicated airstrips and places like empty lots where you won't bother anyone.

A lot of boondockers camp for the solitude and quiet, and may hike and canoe or kayak or bicycle and do other various outdoors activities.

Any kind of solitary pursuit is conducive to the boon-docking life. For example, one boondocking blogger makes his living as a silversmith. He spends most of his time in the backcountry working on craft items, then goes into town and sells his work at galleries and shops. He's one example of someone who has turned a hobby into an oc-cupation.

Any job that you can do on the computer or that in-volves creating something can be done while boondocking. Many people are not retired and have to make a living, and the internet has opened many possibilities for such. Online tutoring is one example, as is providing technical support. But people who use the internet like this are constrained in where they can camp, as they have to have a good connec-tion, though there are ways to boost your internet connec-tion, such as the Wilson antenna.

Writing is another popular hobby among boondockers, some who just write for themselves, and others who actually make a living doing it.

It seems that, like anywhere else, there is a huge variety of people who boondock, each with their own interests. But in general, if you don't have interests, you'll get bored, and this is true whether you boondock or live in a house.

Dealing with Insects, Wild Animals, and Pests

When I first visited the Bugaboos in British Columbia, I was advised to put chicken wire around my vehicle while hiking to keep rodents and porcupines from eating my tires and other rubber components.

I was somewhat incredulous at this, but I've since found that many places in the Rocky Mountains have similar problems. And it's not just in the mountains, for many boondockers in the desert find kangaroo rats and other rodents will climb into their engines and chew on the wires, sometimes rendering them immobile.

Biting and Stinging Insects

Even though I grew up in the Colorado Rockies, I'd never heard of rodents eating wires, but I was familiar with mosquitoes, or so I thought. I was later to find out, once again in Canada, that I knew very little about the pain these and other insects could inflict on an unsuspecting camper. The techniques and devices out there to protect oneself from mosquitoes and flying biters are vast, yet little of it seems to work.

The mosquitoes in the Rockies of Colorado are minor compared to Canada and Alaska's, though they do seem to

be getting worse. And black flies can be even more tortur-
ous, though I have yet to deal with them in numbers. What
Alaskans call "white sox" (black flies) can also torture you,
as they actually climb up under your pantlegs to bite. Blow
flies, midges, no-see-ums, and gnats can all cause allergy
problems (swelling and itching) and make you miserable.

One way to avoid biting insects is to stay away from
their habitat when they're in it. Mosquito season in the
Rockies (including Canada and Alaska) runs approximately
from June or sometimes early July until about mid-August.
This of course depends on things like altitude and whether
or not it's been a wet year, as well as if you're around water
or meadows, where they like to breed.

Once the nights start getting cooler, the numbers seem
to drop off, providing relief. I once camped in a provincial
park in B.C. (Lac la Hache) in late July, where I saw nary
a mosquito, and yet the camp host said he'd literally been
run off by them only a week earlier.

Mosquitos are more active at dawn and dusk, seeming
to settle down during the day, unless you walk through a
grassy meadow or area where they're waiting out the heat.
Most of us don't like the wind, but in mosquito-land it can
be a good thing, as even a breeze will keep their numbers
down. Of course, rain does the same, as can the smoke
from a campfire. This can also apply to other biting insects.

Some people seem more immune to mosquito bites,
and recent research has shown that those with blood type
O are more prone to bites than those with type B. Type A
is the least desirable. It's interesting that type O is also the
universal donor blood type. In addition, about 85 percent
of your susceptibility to bug bites is related to the compo-
sition of your skin bacteria, as well as your levels of lactic

acid, uric acid, ammonia, and other substances present in your sweat.

Mosquitoes can detect carbon dioxide using a special organ (the maxillary palp) from as far as 164 feet away. Since we all emit CO2, mosquitoes will often go for whoever emits the most. Thus, kids are safer when adults are around, and larger adults may get more bites, all other factors being equal.

Things you can do to reduce your attraction:

• Avoid wearing perfume or aftershave. Use unscented soaps and shampoos and even unscented detergent to wash your clothes.

• Avoid alcohol—drinking even just 12 ounces of beer will significantly increase your attraction.

• Don't move much. Visual clues draw mosquitos in. Body heat is also an attractant, but I'm not sure how you could reduce that.

• Wear light colors. These make you less visible to insects.

• Wear headnets and mosquito jackets and pants. I've adapted net jackets with face nets for my dogs for when things are really bad.

• Use bug repellant. DEET seems to be the most effective, but be careful, as some repellants are harmful to plastics and clothing. Permethrin is another, but it should only be put on your clothes.

Some people will liberally apply repellants to their skin, when they should go on your clothing. Some say that Avon's Skin So Soft works, but blind studies have shown it has no effect on mosquitos. Natural Peppermint oil can be put directly on skin and clothing, and some swear by it, as well as lemon eucalyptus, and some like Citronella candles.

Some like electric fly swatters, but this is an active pursuit and as soon as you stop, the bugs return.

If you do get bit, hydrocortisone cream will reduce the itching, as will rubbing alcohol (though it may attract more). I've found that putting alcohol on a swab of cotton and really rubbing it into the spot will seriously reduce the itching.

When camping in a bug-infested area, I've found that having netting on your vehicle windows works wonders, especially if you're sleeping in a van or SUV, where screens aren't standard.

Window netting is easy to make—just buy standard flexible screen material from your hardware store, along with enough magnets to hold it onto the frame of your doors. Cut the screens with plenty left to fold over the door, then use the magnets to hold it on. Some people cut the screens the exact size of the window, but I've found it works better to actually drape the screens over the doorframe, both inside and out, then use magnets for the bottom and sides. This allows you to lower or raise your windows without the screens getting caught in them, and is also more stable. You of course remove this before driving down the road.

Most boondockers own a screen tent, and my favorite is the Clam, as it's easy to put up and take down, as well as to carry around. It's more pricey than most, but will last forever. Cheap screen tents usually don't hold their shape and tend to easily blow away. Be sure to put rocks around the bottom of the tent, as most biting insects are heat-seeking and will find even tiny places to enter.

If you're allergic to bee or wasp stings, be sure to have any necessary medication with you. It also helps to check out where you're going to camp and make sure there aren't any wasp or hornet nests nearby, as well as ant hills. If you end up having a problem with ants, as long as they're not fire ants (which you should never camp near), you can distract them from your camp by giving them a pile of bread crumbs or such to eat on as far away from camp as possible.

Rodents

A number of techniques have been devised to deal with rodents, including putting lights under your hood to deter them, but I suspect the old chicken wire wrap around your vehicle works best, though carrying and setting up the wire can be cumbersome. But it is a guaranteed solution.

When setting up camp, look around for possible nesting areas (leaf litter, branches, shrubs). Ground squirrels leave burrows and sometimes long hummocky underground paths. Rodents, especially packrats, love to eat wiring harnesses, fan belts, and radiator hoses.

Squirrels and chipmunks are seldom a problem, but mice and packrats have an insatiable appetite, especially for thicker wiring, which is sometimes made with soy in the insulating portion. Some people upgrade to silicone wiring and swear that cures the problem.

Another effective solution is to leave your hood open enough to light-up the engine compartment, as rodents don't like light. Propping your hood open a foot or two will discourage them from setting up shop, and some will use a solar flashlight under the hood when it's dark.

Others swear by mothballs, ammonia, dryer sheets, and even Irish Spring soap, as well as cotton balls soaked in peppermint oil. Whatever you try, be sure your pets and children can't get into it (peppermint oil can be toxic, as it contains salicylic acid).

Hantavirus

Hantavirus is a respiratory illness carried by deer mice, and preventative measures can be good if you're camped in their habitat (rural fields, forests, and outbuildings). On that note, I've never heard of anyone getting hantavirus while boondocking, as it's typically associated with confined areas—cabins and sheds inhabited by the mice, who leave their droppings. People tend to get it more while cleaning their old sheds or garages, as sweeping make the virus airborn. Note that house mice are not carriers. There have been outbreaks among campers, but they were typically staying in cabins.

Part of the reason that your odds of getting hantavirus while camping are extremely low is because in a natural setting, mice are kept in check by predators like foxes, raptors, and coyotes. In an outbuilding, the mice can breed unchecked.

In 2012, ten people were infected by hantavirus in Yosemite National Park, with three dying from it. The double-walled tent cabins at the park had become infested and were later destroyed. Tents generally don't provide a place for rodents to live, and the single-walled tents there weren't infested.

Hantavirus has symptoms similar to the flu: chills, muscle aches, fever, headache, dizziness, and fatigue, but the flu goes away after a few days. Hantavirus begins like a simple cold or flu, then after about a week one gets a sudden fever and eventually has trouble breathing. The advance is very rapid and one should immediately get to a doctor if they suspect they may have the virus. People with the virus are not contagious.

Hantavirus is extremely rare, so don't let fear of contracting it slow you down, just be aware and stay aware from confined places with rodent litter. One has to be exposed within 48 hours of the mouse shedding the virus, as the virus can survive for only two days outside a host. And since the virus can live for only two days outside the mouse, the infestation has to be ongoing, not just an occasional mouse passing through.

But if you're boondocking and not digging through rodent nests, the odds are almost zero that you will ever be exposed. I mention it only as something to be aware of.

Valley Fever

Valley Fever is much more common than hantavirus, but your odds of dying from it are much much smaller. But it's also something to be aware of, especially if you're camping in the desert Southwest (including the southern deserts of California). A lot of people who contract it get over it and aren't even aware they've had it, but if your immune system is compromised, it can be deadly. Dogs can also get it.

Valley fever is caused by a fungus that lives in the soils and dust of the Southwest and is contracted when airborne. The fungal spores are microscopic, and the disease is not contagious.

About 40 percent of people who breathe in the spore have no symptoms, which can include fatigue, fever, a cough, headache, night sweats, muscle aches, rash, and shortness of breath. In serious cases, the fever can lead to pneumonia and even meningitis, though rare. Over 65 percent of all cases occur in Arizona, and 30 percent occur in California, with 5 percent in Nevada, southwestern Utah, and New Mexico.

Your odds of contracting Valley Fever are higher if you have diabetes or a compromised immune system. It's difficult to avoid it in these areas, but not digging in the soil and staying indoors during dust storms will lower your odds.

Is this a reason to avoid some of the best and only winter boondocking spots in the U.S.? Many people with respiratory problems, such as asthma, find relief only by living in warm places like Arizona. If you're in a city, your odds of getting Valley Fever are less, but you might be better off going to Florida.

I personally had a friend die from Valley Fever (he lived in a house in Phoenix) and am probably more cautious than most because of that, but it actually kills few people, and once you've had it, you're immune to it, as long as you actually get over it, for its effects can be long-lasting. But if you have a compromised immune system, you might be wise to consider it before heading south.

Wild Animals

Everyone's seen or heard stories about Yosemite bears breaking into cars, or maybe you've read about the occasional grizzly deaths in Yellowstone and western Montana.

We're all afraid of apex predators, thus the on-going campaigns to exterminate them from Earth. Much of this push is from those who raise stock, but the rest of us are also typically afraid of bears, mountain lions, and wolves, though wolves have rarely been responsible for a human death. Some people are afraid of coyotes, who are even less likely to attack a human than is a wolf.

When you're out camping, especially alone, I can guarantee that things that go bump in the night are even more worrisome than when in a house. Ironically, you're statistically safer when camping than when in a house, especially when boondocking, for your main enemy is actually other humans, not predators. If something were to happen to you in the backcountry, odds are best that it would be from something you did yourself (carelessness with guns, accidents, etc.) or from another human. (I'll talk about safety later.)

In general, predators aren't really even a factor when boondocking, except when it comes to your pets, which you should never leave outside alone at night, as even large dogs can be coyote bait. I've woken to mountain lion tracks around my tent, had bears look through my trailer windows, and even met up with bears, coyotes, and mountain lions on the trail, and they have always run away.

But the secret is to never assume they will run away, and to thus be prepared. If you're in bear country, always carry bear spray, even around camp. Some carry air horns, but bear spray has proven to be effective, and air horns haven't. Studies by Montana State University have shown bear spray is more effective than carrying a gun. Hike with your dogs on leash only, as a dog can quickly chase after a bear and then bring them back to you, which has been the cause of a number of maulings.

If you're in mountain lion country, be aware and never let your pets run loose unless they always stay in camp and you're there watching them. In all honesty, your pets are at a much greater risk than you ever will be. It goes without saying that children should never be left unattended in or out of camp.

Most predators are even more leery of us than we are of them, though there are places where wildlife is becoming more used to people and losing their fear, which usually doesn't end well for the animals. It's highly unlikely a bear would try to break into your trailer, unless it's hungry and can smell food, so it's always best to cook outside and store your food in your vehicle when in bear country. If you're tent camping, this is even more critical. Keeping your food secured and having a clean camp is probably the most effective bear deterrent there is.

In general, if you're careful with your food and don't go blindly into their habitat (as in hiking into places where bears are likely to bed down), your odds of even seeing a predator are slim, especially wolves, and mountain lions are elusive to the point that most people consider it a treat to see one (of course when from a distance and not up close). If you do see a bear or lion, turn around and go the opposite direction, keeping as great a distance from them as possible. Avoid eye contact and never run. Be sure you know how to use your bear spray (it will work on other animals besides bears, including humans), and be aware that most bear charges are bluff charges.

Interestingly enough, the very wild animals that often do the most damage are typically not perceived to be dangerous. Moose kill more people than bears and lions combined, and even elk and deer can injure or kill you.

Because wolves are the mortal enemy of moose and eat their young, moose hate dogs, and a number of moose attacks on people were precipitated by the moose going after the person's dog. Moose are unpredictable, peacefully grazing one minute and chasing you the next. The good thing about animals such as moose, elk, deer, and bison (buffalo) is that they're not predatory and are generally happy once you leave their area, so your goal is to simply get away as fast as you can if threatened by one.

All of these animals have been known to kill wolves, lions, and bears, which means they can be lethal with their hooves. And on top of that, they are all much faster than you. Your best defense is to stay away from them, and if you are chased, put something between you and them, even if it's just a tree. Be especially careful if there are young present.

This doesn't mean you can't go out and enjoy nature, just be prudent and aware. Keep your distance from wild animals, keep a clean camp, and always carry bear spray.

So, don't let a fear of wild animals keep you from boondocking.

Snakes, Scorpions, and Creepy Crawlies

Like most other critters, rattlesnakes don't like humans and will usually go the other direction, unless you catch them by surprise, and even then, they can tell you're not prey and will often not strike. But the greatest danger from poisonous snakes is to children and pets, as their smaller size means they're more susceptible to the venom, and children are more likely to be checking out the places where snakes live, such as holes and hidden areas.

Even if they do strike, only about 50 percent will inject venom, which is rarely fatal to a healthy adult. An average of six people a year die in the U.S. from snake bite, and that includes the south, where copperheads and other poisonous snakes are more common. One demographic study some years ago found that over 98 percent of bite victims are young adult males, and over 80 percent of those had a blood alcohol level above the legal limit for driving.

The best first-aid kit for snakebite is a set of car keys—get into the nearest ER immediately. The best way to not get bit involves mostly just watching where you walk. If you are in rattlesnake country, be aware of when they hibernate and when they're most awake when not in hibernation, which is typically in the morning and evening hours in summer, when it's cooler. By knowing when they're most active and where they're most likely to hang out, you can avoid them without too much trouble.

Dogs are a different matter and should be kept on leash during times and in places where snakes are likely. A canine preventative anti-venom is available from vets, which requires getting shots before being bitten, but there is a lot of controversy as to whether it actually works or not. Snake-avoidance training is available in places where snakes are most common, such as parts of Arizona, and is probably more effective in the long run than the anti-venom shots.

There are plenty of places where snakes flourish, and your best bet is to know whether or not they may be around where you camp. I've spent literally months in hot deserts where I would expect to see lots of snakes and seen nary a one, yet have seen them the first day I was in a cool grassy meadow in Montana. I actually prefer country that's more arid, as it's easier to see snakes, since there's less vegetation. I do have a snakebite kit, but have never had to use it, fortunately.

Be sure to always empty your shoes and anything a snake might crawl into before you use it. Also, never reach into dark hidden places.

The closest I've ever come to a rattler was walking down a wash in Canyonlands National Park where I ran into a midget rattler, which are very toxic, and it and I both went our separate directions as fast as possible. The best course of action in such cases is preventative, as I mentioned before—don't go walking down desert washes in the cool evening hours.

One problem with warmer climates is that scorpions and other semi-dangerous critters are more common. Most are easily avoided by not sleeping on the ground and by always carefully checking things before picking them up, such as wood for your campfire. Wearing gloves can help prevent stings.

Most creepy crawlies are nocturnal, which means you will never know they're around unless you go out at night looking for them. I had a friend give me a blacklight not too long ago and was shocked to see my entire camp was infested with scorpions. I had been there for months (as a camp host) and never seen even one. I was a lot more careful afterwards, but it probably wouldn't have mattered, as they hadn't bothered me a bit. As with most things, common sense is good (don't run around barefoot). I gave the light to a visiting class of young kids, who had a ball with it.

Spiders can cause painful bites, but are rarely poisonous. Black widows seem to live in many climates and places, but they're typically reclusive and keep to themselves in dark hidden places. I think I would rather see a snake than a black widow, but each of us has different tolerances. Studies with very young children indicate that most people either abhor snakes or spiders but not both, and it appears to be a a genetic disposition as to which it is.

Some kinds of centipedes can be lethal, but they're rare and are, once again, further south. Parts of Utah and the desert southwest have Giant Desert Centipedes, which have a very painful bite, and their looks may cause a heart attack, as they can get big and are very fuzzy. I saw one once that was easily a foot long, but it was at night out on a remote dirt road where I was walking my dogs by flashlight after a long day of driving. When I lived in Moab, Utah, my cat used to bring them into the house, which was a very unpleasant experience.

Keep in mind that the majority of such critters you can also encounter when you live in a house, whether in your yard or inside the house itself. When you're boondocking, you can always leave such places, whereas in a house, you can't.

In short, dealing with pests and predators is like most other things—use a good dose of common sense and you'll find you'll rarely, if ever, have a problem.

Safety and Security

When it comes to safety and security, most boondockers have two concerns: how can I make sure I'm safe out in the boonies, and how can I make sure my rig and equipment are secure when I go for a hike or leave them to drive into town?

Both are valid concerns, and of course how concerned you should be depends on where you camp. If you're in a campground or RV park, safety and security are much less of an issue, though equipment can and does disappear in these supposedly more secure settings. But if you're boondocking in an area that sees lots of traffic (ATVs, hikers, etc.), you may want to exercise certain cautions.

In my experience, as well as from talking to others, I believe that the further you are from people, the safer you and your stuff are. The odds of being robbed seem to decrease the further one gets from pavement. It makes sense that if no one knows you're there, you're not likely to have anyone steal anything. One boondocker I know has a basic rule that says to camp ten miles from town, a mile from pavement, and out of sight of graded or graveled roads.

It may seem counterintuitive, but you really are more secure out boondocking than in most campgrounds, unless you're in a private campground where the owners watch everyone who comes and goes like hawks (and these do exist, but being watched can get a little old).

If you camp near a large urban area, the odds are much better that your stuff is at risk than if you camp in a rural area. Of course, all it takes is one dishonest person, no matter where you are, so it's always prudent to keep your stuff secure. I generally believe that you're safer boondocking than about anywhere if you take the right precautions (the above distance rule being one).

Sometimes you want to run into town but don't want to leave your stuff sitting for several hours. If you have a trailer, things are a little easier, because you can just put anything valuable inside your trailer and lock it. This assumes, of course, that no one will break into your trailer, but things will be somewhat safer, as the less effort it takes to take something, the better the odds it will be stolen.

But safety can be a concern no matter where you camp. I have some friends who usually exclusively boondock, but ended up staying in a Walmart parking lot for a couple of nights in a medium-sized city. They got up one morning to find their mountain bikes, which they'd locked to their rig, gone. This was after they had boondocked for weeks and never even locked their bikes.

Again, some things are just common sense, such as taking your expensive computer gear with you when you go into town instead of leaving it in your trailer. If you camp in a tent, this is even more critical. Some people I know just never buy nice things. If they get a camp chair, they'll get a cheap one instead of the nice one, so if it is stolen, it's not much of a loss.

In general, where I camp, it's unusual to have anything stolen, although this will vary by location. But where I generally camp, in Utah, Colorado, and Montana, there are fewer people, so your stuff is generally safer. But it's always a good idea to take anything you would regret losing with you when you leave your camp, if possible.

As they say, a lock keeps an honest person honest. So, lock everything that could walk away while you're gone. I have a suitcase solar panel, and when I leave I will either put a bolt lock on it, locking it to my trailer tire rim, or I may even just put it inside the trailer. I don't bother to put away my camp chair and rug and table and things like that, but I do have a heavy duty hitch lock that I put on my trailer—not the kind that can be removed with bolt cutters, but the kind that takes a torch.

Some parts of the country are so crowded that I would always lock everything. And if I'm in border areas, such as places in southern California, Arizona, and New Mexico, I would always lock everything. But my general philosophy is why camp where you have to be nervous about such things, because if you're worried about things being stolen, then there are usually too many people around. I tend to gravitate to places that are way out in the boonies.

There are little things you can do to make people think you're home or soon will be. For example, you can leave a note that says something like, "Hi Jerry, sorry I missed you, but stick around, as I'm just over the hill rockhounding. Jim should be back any minute, as he ran into town for groceries."

How effective something like this would be I don't know, but I do know boondockers who do it.

It goes without saying that the nicer your stuff, the more likely you will be to have it stolen. I have friends who camp in old beat-up pickups and never lock anything no matter where they are and have never had anything stolen—but I also have friends with nice shiny new rigs who have never had anything stolen.

After years of boondocking, I can thankfully say I've never had even one thing stolen. I've found that, in general, people in the backcountry tend to be fellow campers and respect other people's camps. Of course, the closer you camp to a busy road, the higher your odds of losing something, although this doesn't mean you should spend all your time worrying about it.

One thing I will never leave in my camp is one of my pets. Some people will leave their dog or cat in their trailer, but I would never do this unless in a secure campground. A trailer can be replaced, but a pet can't. If my cats are camping with me, I have carriers in my car, and they always go along with me, and this also gives me the peace of mind of knowing they're not getting too hot or too cold in my trailer. This does limit me, of course, as they can get hot in the vehicle.

I know of one fellow who camps full-time and tends to carry cash with him rather than have a bank card. When he leaves camp, he hides the money under a rock or someplace most would never think of looking for money. That way, he figures if someone breaks into his trailer they won't find his cash, nor will they if they break into his car. Whether this is a good idea or not I can't say, as I would forget where I hid it.

Camping in groups can be a deterrent unless you all leave at the same time. It doesn't necessarily follow that someone won't be as likely to steal, as some see it as more of an opportunity where they can burglarize many rigs at once.

But like most things with boondocking, it just depends on where you are. The campground in southeast Utah where I sometimes serve as camp host has approximately 130 campsites, all spread apart where often you can't see anyone else from your camp spot. Because it's an area where people tend to be gone all day hiking, mountain biking, climbing, or exploring, often there's virtually no one in a camp for hours on end. And yet, through the last 10 years, you can literally count on one hand the number of thefts. So, it does depend on where you are.

Some like to make their town runs during the midweek, as there are typically fewer people around than on the weekends.

Some people swear by motion detectors (driveway alarms) that alert them when someone is coming down the road where they're camped. These alert you to possible intruders, and in my mind serve more as a personal safety device rather than to deter thieves, but if it's dark outside, it's nice to know if someone's around. Motion detector lights also will alert you, but the intruder isn't usually a human, but is more likely to be a deer or other critter.

Another method is to make a line in the dirt across the road as you leave. If it has tread marks when you return, you know someone has entered your camp. This might be helpful in making you more aware, especially if the line has been crossed only once. Some actually even use game cameras around camp.

Some solo campers have techniques they use to make people think they're not alone, such as putting two or three chairs in their camp space, as well as extra boots by the door and even a dog bowl or tie-out.

Some like to put "Beware of Dog" signs in their windows, along with signs that advertise guns and gun-club memberships (think NRA). Does this help any? I have no idea, but it does advertise that you may have valuable guns inside to steal.

Many will disagree, but letting on that you're afraid may not be the best preventative measure, and it also indicates you may have something of value inside. Those who live in inner cities ridden with crime often leave their car doors unlocked and windows open advertising they have nothing to steal, so they don't have their cars destroyed by crooks. And some believe that signs advertising you have guns may give the police motive to stop and search you.

Who really knows? I have yet to read any hard statistics for having or not having such signs or stickers, so take it or leave it and do what you feel is best.

It probably is better to not have a sign indicating who's inside or where you live (the Robertsons from Las Vegas). Such signs show you're a friendly tourist, and those days of trusting one another are pretty much gone for many, sadly enough.

Some boondockers like to get everything done before dark, such as walking the dogs, so they can go inside where they're secure. There's nothing wrong with this except you're often missing out on one of the joys of boondock-ing—the beautiful starry skies.

Keep in mind that your best antidote to fear is turning off your news source, as the media will and does report every bad thing that happens, and now that national affairs are so easy to follow, we're inundated with bad news, mak-ing it feel like the world is getting less and less safe. If you have 20 bad things happening a day across the country, you can guarantee they'll make the news, and it will seem more like they all happened nearby, though they were spread across millions of people and thousands of miles.

Guns

I grew up in a culture (western Colorado) where guns were a fairly politically neutral item, as people hunted but rarely shot each other. Nobody cared much if you had a gun and it was even expected that you probably did, though nobody talked much about it.

Things have changed, and guns have become a very controversial topic. If you want to shut down a thread on an internet forum, just make a post about guns. It won't be long before everyone's arguing about them in a manner that makes you glad they're not all in the same room to-gether and have guns.

I grew up learning to target shoot, but never was one for hunting, as I love animals. I carried a small .22 pistol for years, and only recently gave it away. I never used it, and if I had needed it, I would probably be a goner long before I could find it, as I usually kept it hidden away.

I'm of the frame of mind that safety is more a matter of being aware of one's surroundings than owning guns, and

I also think dogs are a great deterrent, especially the kind of dogs I have, Australian cattle dogs, which are very loyal. Having dogs will make you a harder target.

If you feel safer with a gun, by all means get a gun, but you should know how to properly use it and whether or not you really could shoot someone. How would you know until the time came, and then, if you find out you can't, odds are good the other person will take your gun and shoot you with it. In addition, gun accidents aren't that uncommon and often involve a family member who was thought to be a burglar. And a bullet can penetrate objects you would rather they didn't, like your neighbor's RV or car or even your neighbor himself (and they don't have to be all that close).

And if you do shoot someone, even in self-defense, be prepared to hire an attorney to prove it was justifiable, or you'll be going to prison. To me, no possession is worth killing someone over, and the majority of would-be assailants are after your stuff. Keep in mind also that many criminals are very adept at knowing how to disarm others.

I have yet to talk with another boondocker who felt guns were necessary or who had used one successfully for a security problem.

It's human nature to assume most people are reasonable, but there are definitely people out there who are deranged and mentally unstable. Just be assured that you're less likely to meet them when out in the sticks, but if you do, be prepared mentally in what you'll do. I have yet to meet anyone I felt uncomfortable around enough to move camp and leave, but I've always been prepared to do so.

Situational awareness is critical when dealing with others, and displaying confidence and knowing when not to argue will serve you well. I've never had to give up my camp or possessions, but I would if I needed to. But if it came to needing to actually defend myself, I would prefer to use bear spray or mace over a gun, as it's much easier to deploy and works great, with no long-term damage. Bats, fire extinguishers, air horns, and even using your key fob to turn on your car alarm can all be used for self-protection.

And when it comes to guns and protection against large animals, many gun owners just aren't very familiar with how to shoot a gun in a situation of high stress. Bears can run 30 m.p.h. and are often on you before you can even think about getting or using a gun. Bear spray takes very little training and is also effective against people.

Personal Locator Beacons

I always carry a personal locator beacon (PLB) and consider it the most critical item in potentially saving my life or even the lives of others. PLBs have been used in about every situation imaginable and will activate a satellite signal that tells search and rescue you need help. There are very few places they won't work (caves and some deep slot canyons).

Other devices such as the SPOT Satellite Messenger are popular but require monthly service fees. PLBs can be purchased on-line and from places like REI and outdoor shops and typically cost only a couple of hundred dollars, well worth it if you need a rescue.

And it's good to purchase state rescue insurance if the state you frequent has it. For example, Colorado has an annual license one can purchase for just a few dollars that ensures you won't be charged if you need a rescue. Some areas won't charge if you're a resident. SAR fees can be hefty, especially if a helicopter rescue is necessary. Many private helicopter services now also offer insurance for emergencies. (I cover more on PLBs in the Sickness and Health Emergencies chapter.)

Other Tips

Other safety tips include keeping your vehicle in good repair so you control where and when you stop. When you find a good spot, scout it out and see how it feels. Trust your intuition and leave if it doesn't feel right, even if there's no logical explanation. If someone around you doesn't feel right, leave. Most boondockers are good folks, but there are unbalanced people everywhere. If you are camped near others, take the time to go say hello. People who know each other, even in a cursory way, tend to look out for and be less fearful of each other.

Make sure someone knows where you are and will keep an eye out for you, if possible. SPOT devices are good for this, as one can send text messages, as well as allow others to track them.

Forest Fires and Flashfloods

It goes without saying that in some places, such as the desert, fires aren't much of a concern, but a lot of people enjoy camping in the national forests, where forest fires can mean possible death if you're caught in one. And camping along a creek won't necessarily save you, as fires are becoming hotter and moving faster as drought becomes more and more common.

If you're camped in an area that has the internet, you can check http://inciweb.nwcg.gov for the latest updates on fires, but this site, accurate as it is, often doesn't show a fire until it's become a certain size, so if you're in the path of a small fire, you may not see it there.

Because many fires are caused by lightning strikes, camping on a ridge or in a place with good views might give you a good view of smoke, but this also can make you more vulnerable to getting hit by lightning yourself. It goes without saying that if you can smell or see smoke, you would be prudent to investigate and/or be ready to leave.

If you're camped in an established campground, odds are good you'll be told to evacuate by rangers or law enforcement before a fire arrives, but not always, as some fires simply move too fast. But when boondocking, you're pretty much on your own.

I know some boondockers who no longer light campfires for fear of setting the forest on fire, as things have become so dry in many areas. One can always buy a propane campfire if you really want to have a fire, which is probably the safest way to do it.

Another concern is flashfloods, and the most deadly ones are generally in areas where it's difficult for water to quickly soak into the ground, such as in Zion National Park and many parts of Utah (Canyonlands, Arches, Capitol Reef, etc.). But in other areas, where the water can soak in, flash floods can still be a danger once the ground is saturated. Flashfloods often occur when storms sit in one place for an inordinate amount of time, such as the tragic flood in Big Thompson Canyon in Colorado. Debris flows and mudslides can also occur.

Never camp in a wash or obvious drainage, no matter how good the weather looks, as flashflood waters can come from miles away. Never try to cross water more than two-feet deep, as that's all it takes to float your vehicle if the flow is high enough. Having said this, yes, there are times it's fine to cross, as with a mountain creek that has a good visible gravel bottom that's not flowing rapidly—the two-foot number is a general rule of thumb.

It can also be dangerous to camp even in low spots, as enough rain will create standing pools of water that may not wash you away, but will certainly get you wet and possibly even stuck. And be aware of the kind of dirt you're camped on—if it's sand, you're probably OK (if you're not in a drainage), but most clays will become slippery when wet and impassible.

The best preparation you can have for bad weather is getting a NOAA weather radio and listening to it often. Be sure it's battery powered or, better yet, solar and/or crank powered. NOAA radios will give you the general weather forecast as well as hazard and emergency warnings for your area.

In general, safety and security often depend more on where you set up camp than anything else, so be prudent and camp in areas that feel safe to you—your instincts are valuable and good indicators. You can also ask police, locals, and forestry and BLM workers in the nearest town what areas are best to avoid.

Fear can be paralyzing, but the more you get out and camp, the less irrational fear you will have. Your first few nights out may be uncomfortable, but the more you boon-dock, the more you'll realize that your common sense and caution will make you actually safer than you might be in civilization—and the scenery's usually better, too.

The following things will help ensure your safety:

• Trust your instincts.

• Be confident and self-assured around others.

• Don't share personal information with people you first meet or tell them where you're camped.

• Be sure family or a friend knows where you're camped and your itinerary, but don't put it on social media until after the fact and you're not there any longer.

• Don't tell others you're a solo traveler.

• Park your rig so you can drive away if need be.

• Keep your rig in good repair and have emergency items handy, such as a fire extinguisher, battery cables, a portable air compressor, and tools to fix a flat.

• Keep bear spray handy, even in your car, and always lock your car/rig when in it, especially if you don't have dogs to alert you when someone's nearby.

• Carry a first-aid kit.

• Always have an extra key to your vehicle and your trailer/rig hidden where only you can find it.

• If in a questionable area, don't leave valuables out-side, even while you're in the rig, without locking them. Put them inside when gone.

• If your vehicle has a GPS, don't use it as your primary source of directions. Always verify where you're going with a map so you don't end up lost or somewhere you don't want to be. GPS units are not always reliable.

• Always carry a personal locator beacon (PLB), especially when hiking, as well as a first-aid kit and cell phone (keep it charged) and a flashlight.

• Carry extra food and water and a weather radio.

• Carry something in your car and rig to break out the windows and cut a seat belt, and have them handy. You will hopefully never need them, but if you do, you'll be happy you have them.

• Be aware of the weather and don't camp in areas that could be unsafe in rainy weather or impossible to get out of if there's a fire.

• Don't advertise your presence by putting outside lights on your rig or leaving your porch light on at night. Some set up driveway alarms to let them know when someone is coming. Motion detector lights can also be helpful.

• Lock everything you would hate to lose.

Sickness and Health Emergencies

One thing people worry about, especially when camping alone, is getting sick or injured and not having anyone to help them. This is, of course, particularly worrisome if one has pets.

The first thing you should do is to keep a supply of things handy that you might need if you do get sick. This could include things like chicken broth, echinacea tea, and the kinds of medicines that one would take for flues and colds or anything you may be more susceptible to.

It's also very important that you run a tight ship, so to speak, so that if you are sick you're not as likely to have to do chores that you've put off. Keeping plenty of water and propane and that kind of thing on hand falls under that topic. This is one reason I like to keep a bit ahead on my supplies and not wait until the last minute to replenish my water supply and food.

Of course, if you suspect that you're going to get really sick, for example, you've been around a friend who had a severe flu and you feel like you're catching it, it might be prudent to load everything up and go into town or to a friend's while you can.

Most boondockers have some form of communication, usually a cell phone, and can call a friend or relative if they feel like things are going downhill and they need help. This is another reason that solo boondockers will often tend to group up and camp with birds of the same feather. Of course, if you have a spouse or partner, it's easier, as they can help look out for you if you're sick or injured.

To me, being injured is more of a concern than is getting sick. An injury can happy quickly and be life-threatening. For example, you could be out hiking and twist an ankle or break a leg, making it impossible for you to get back to camp. And even though the common wisdom says to never hike alone, many of us love solitude and often do hike alone.

Assuming you have a cell phone signal, this is when a cell phone is worth its weight in gold. I prefer the little flip phones, as you can just stick them in your shirt or jeans pocket, whereas the larger tablet type phones are more difficult to carry. Like bear spray, you always need to have your cell phone within handy reach. A whistle can help if you're in an area where others hike.

The one device everyone should have and carry consistently is a personal locator beacon, or PLB. They're easy to purchase and can be bought online for under $250, and if you read the stories on the internet about the numerous lives they've saved, you'll be convinced that they're one of the most important purchases you'll ever make, whether you camp or not. Everyone should also have one in their car.

PLB's are small, much like a flip phone, and can easily be carried in your pocket. Once activated, they send a signal to one of a number of satellites that are constantly circling the earth, and that signal is then forwarded to the Air Force Search and Rescue Center. They then contact your local search and rescue organization with the necessary information to instigate a search.

Be aware that a PLB rescue can often be a lengthy matter, as the satellites are not necessarily always above you and it may take 30 minutes to transmit a signal, and then sometimes a number of hours to actually get someone to your location.

A PLB is not something you use for minor injuries like a sprained ankle, but should be reserved for life-threatening events. And the life you save may not necessarily be your own, but may be someone else's. There have been a number of cases where someone with a PLB happened upon someone seriously injured and used the device to summon help.

Along these lines, it's helpful to carry a hiking pole with you, not just for making hiking easier, but it can serve as a sort of crutch if you happen to sprain your ankle.

Probably one of the most common problems in the backcountry, no matter what you're doing, whether biking, hiking, etc., is dehydration. People tend to not carry enough water or drink enough and eventually can suffer heat stroke.

If the weather's cooler, hypothermia can become a concern, where your body cannot keep its core warm and begins to shut down. It doesn't have to be extremely cold for this to happen, and a lot of hypothermia happens when it's even as warm as 50°. It's critical to dress for the weather and carry extra clothing with you. The initial symptoms of hypothermia are confusion and shivering.

What about your pets in the case that you become sick or injured? This is a very serious concern for most boondockers, as it seems the majority of campers do have pets.

Some wear a bracelet that has their own medical information as well as information about their pets and who to contact. Some will carry a laminated card in their pocket or wallet, as this is the first place an EMT crew will check. A laminated card may be good for basic information, but you also need to let the authorities know where your pets are located if you left them behind, so another card that you update as needed would be good. You can include the GPS location of your rig as well.

I have a piece of paper taped to the inside wall of my rig by the front door that states the number of pets I have, their names, medical issues (if any), and who to contact about their care if something happens to me. It's good if someone needs to break into my rig to rescue them, but otherwise isn't much help.

For peace of mind, you might consider the services that Good Sam and other insurance companies offer that will guarantee you and your pets care and safe travel after an accident. These services will take care of your rig if you're sick and need hospitalization, making sure it's in safe storage or wherever you want it to be, as well as making sure your pets are cared for.

One nice thing about being sociable is that making friends with other RVers can help guarantee that you know people who will help you, assuming they're in the same area. Even strangers can be immensely helpful, and I've read many stories about people going above and beyond for people they didn't even know. In general, I think people like to help and are kind. Be sure to pay such things forward.

It's also prudent to have emergency roadside service, even though it often won't cover you if you're off on some backroad. Be sure it will cover towing both your rig and trailer if that's the setup you have. Sometimes it will cover taking your trailer to an RV park, providing you with a place to live while your tow vehicle is under repair.

It's important that you eat healthy foods and continue to exercise, no matter where you are, but in general, your odds of getting injured or sick are lower as a boondocker, as you'll hopefully be off somewhere in the boonies away from people carrying viruses and far away from vehicles with crazy drivers.

Responsible Camping

It's important to remember that boondocking brings with it a level of environmental responsibility, and one should always leave a camp better than they found it. If you don't, the garbage or destruction you find upon returning will likely be yours.

It can take years for nature to recover from one thoughtless camper, and irresponsible campers are often the reason that overused areas get closed.

Follow the maxims of leave no trace, make no new roads or trails, pack out everything, stay off fragile lands, and don't pollute the water.

Most public lands restrict your stay to a maximum of 14 days, and even though you may never see a soul during your stay, there will be others using your spot behind you. If you leave a mess, odds are good others will add to it, and eventually you'll return to find the place closed to camping. This has happened to many places, one example being Florida's Ocala National Forest, which no longer allows boondocking, as well as much of the land around Moab, Utah, Flagstaff, Arizona, and many other popular places.

If you do choose to camp in a place that has trash, it would be good to pack it out, even though you didn't make the mess. The people who choose to trash an area are making sure their kids and grandkids won't be able to go camping, as everything will be closed. Consider packing out a little trash as the price you pay to stay for free in some of the most magnificent areas in the country.

Land management agencies get flak for closing areas, yet good conservation is in the land's best interest, and it's also in the interest of the U.S. public to want our areas managed properly and not trashed. Part of being a good boondocker is to not destroy or damage the environment you're living in, just as you wouldn't want your yard trashed if you lived in a house.

In addition to picking up whatever garbage is around your site, being a responsible boondocker also means having respect for those around you.

In an ideal situation, you won't have neighbors, but if you do, be respectful of their privacy and don't run your generator at odd hours or blast your music and talk loud during quiet hours when people might be sleeping. Most of us boondock to get away from noise and other people and to enjoy nature.

Another aspect of responsible camping is to be sure you're camped in an area that's legal and open to the public. Sometimes an area may be closed for revegetation or because it's a wildlife calving or nesting area. Always respect signs telling you to stay off, and even if there's no sign, use your best judgement as to whether a place is a sensitive area for wildlife (such as a wetlands).

Space Invaders

As I write this, there's a pickup pulling a trailer with mountain bikes on the bumper coming up the road, and I'm watching them intently to see if they will continue on or decide to try to stop and share my camp spot.

One of my main concerns about boondocking is invaders, uninvited people who want to share your spot. The last thing most boondockers want is company, and yet many campers think it's okay to invade other people's privacy.

I would guess that most people who boondock do so because they enjoy solitude and privacy, not because it's free—the free part is the icing on the cake.

It never fails that, for example, when you're in a campground, you pull way over to the furthest corner in the back, and even if the campground is otherwise empty, you'll soon have someone camping right next to you. This even happens when you're camped in places like Cracker Barrel, Flying J, or Walmart.

Space invaders illustrate the human need to group together and the belief that there's safety in numbers. If you happen to camp in an area with space around you, you may end up surrounded by people, the very thing you came to the backcountry to get away from.

So, what do you do about invaders? It depends somewhat on where you camp, and it seems like invaders are less likely when you're way out in the back country. Generally, the people who camp in the back country are more likely to also be wanting solitude and will find their own isolated camp spots.

This is not always the case, though. I recently met up with some friends who had been camped in a very remote part of Utah and were surprised one night to have a motorhome pull up right smack next to them, even though there were literally thousands and thousands of acres all around where that party could have camped.

The next morning, upon getting to know their new neighbors better, they found that they were afraid of being alone in the backcountry. This seemed somewhat ironic to my friends.

Some areas are traditional to families that have lived nearby for a long time, and they will come out and camp whether you're there or not, especially during holidays like the Fourth of July. I've heard many tales of a happy camper suddenly being surrounded in wagon train fashion by a group who always camps there at a certain time of the year and will not let one lone camper stop them. In their minds, you're the invader, and sometimes it's better to move or go with the flow and be sociable.

So, what do you do to prevent invaders? Well, as mentioned, the most obvious thing is to camp as far away from civilization as possible, in places were very few people ever go. But barring that, there are other techniques one can employ to reduce the odds of a invader invasion.

One technique is to spread out your camp as much as possible, making it look like there are more people there. This may include things such as carrying a few extra camp chairs with you and setting them strategically about, and dragging your stuff around so it looks like lots of people are there. I myself have often set up an extra tent and made it look like there were other people camped nearby.

If you're camped in a spot where people really can't tell if you're there or not, such as down a two-track road in the trees, or around a small hill, you can do certain things to tell them you're back there so they don't drive down there in the first place. I've taken a big piece of cardboard and written the word "full" on it and placed it in the road with a rock or two to hold it, and I think most people would respect this and not come down the road looking for a camp spot.

But sometimes it doesn't seem like there's much you can do to stop invaders. I remember one time when I was camped in a remote area with literally acre after acre of camp spots all around when a pickup full of guys camped not more than 100 feet from me. It was evening and I was tent camping, so what could I do? I wasn't about to pick up my heavy canvas tent and try to relocate my camp that late in the day.

They were quiet during the night, but the next morning, bright and early, they started skeet shooting. This scared my dogs to death, and after I got them into my car, I did pick up camp and pull stakes. Sometimes it's best to just cut your losses, tuck it in, and move.

Another thing you can do is select camp spots that have obstacles to get through to reach them, as even things like a big mud puddle will deter many campers. Some people will put a large sign in the window of their rig that says "Vicious Dog," but I don't know if this really helps or not.

I've often wondered why people who are afraid to camp bother to go camping, but invaders prove such folks are alive and well. And typically, I've found that people who will invade your camp will also invade your privacy by making noise, letting their dogs and kids run amok, and also by often leaving their trash behind. It seems that considerate people typically just aren't space invaders.

But whatever you do, it's best to avoid confrontation. Sometimes if you go talk to an invader as they're setting up camp and explain why you would prefer they go somewhere else, you will have good results, if you do it in a nice way. It helps if you can point them to another camp spot. But sometimes it just makes them mad.

As a camp host, I've had to mediate many arguments over camp spots where one party would infringe on the other, sometimes even parking their vehicle in their neighbor's spot, and it always amazed me at how inconsiderate some people can be. I've even had campers set up extensive camps in my own site, even though my trailer and Camp Host sign were there. But when you're a camp host, you can always call a ranger if need be.

I recall a time when I was camped way out in the backcountry and a camper came in around 10 p.m. and started to set up camp next to me, even though, once again, there were literally almost infinite places to camp in the area. I kindly told them that I was waiting for a bunch of Boy Scouts to arrive and they probably wouldn't get any sleep if they camped there, then pointed out another campsite down the road a mile or so. They seemed very appreciative, and I couldn't help but laugh about my fictional boy-scout troop.

I guess I'll go to any length to preserve my privacy, but the best way to do so is to camp as far out as possible and pick a spot that has room only for your own camp. And sometimes I live by the old Chinese saying, "Live where no one else wants to live," picking sites that most people wouldn't want, such as in an abandoned gravel pit or out in the middle of a scrub sagebrush flat.

When you want peace and quiet, sometimes that's the best way to find it.

Finding Good Campsites and Staying Legal

Since most of my boondocking has been in the western U.S., as well as Canada and Alaska, let me say up front that I have little familiarity with boondocking in the rest of the country. I've never tried boondocking in the East, the Midwest, or the South, which is a significant portion of our great land. But since most of the 650 million acres of public land is in the western states, I would guess that most serious boondockers head out West.

However, having said that, I'll add that most boondocking basics will be the same no matter where you are, including finding good sites, as the methods won't differ. However, finding boondocking sites is a lot more difficult in places without large expanses of public lands.

What are Public Lands?

Public lands, by definition, belong to the citizens of the United States and are administered for us by various agencies, including the BLM (Bureau of Land Management), USFS (U.S. Forest Service), the Bureau of Reclamation, and the U.S. Army Corp. of Engineers. There are other federal agencies, but these will be the ones you are most likely to engage with, whither directly or indirectly, and with the BLM and USFS managing most of our public lands.

The lands managed by each of these entities is divided into districts, and each district will have its own headquarters, typically with public offices where one can talk to rangers and get maps and other pertinent information. I have yet to go into a district office where the people have been anything but friendly and helpful, and some offices even have their own regional bookstores and educational displays.

Various field offices may also exist, depending on the district, and these can also be helpful. Such offices are an excellent source of maps and advice about the rules and where to boondock. Making a stop in one can save you a lot of trial and error.

Public lands all have rules and regulations for camping, though some areas will have more enforcement than others. It's up to you to know the rules for each district and to follow them, but in general, most public lands restrict camping to 14 days in one spot, and then you have to move a set distance away for a designated time before you can return to that same spot.

The number of days is what typically varies between districts, and this is a function usually of the amount of public usage an area gets. Thus, never assume that the rules stay the same, as they don't, and the penalties each district has for breaking them may also vary.

Squatters

One thing all potential boondockers must know up front, a fact that will be critical to your future plans, is that as the economy varies, so does the number of people living on public lands.

When the economy is bad, you're going to see more people living in the boonies by necessity, and as these numbers increase, so will the attempts by law enforcement to decrease their impact by trying to get them to move on to somewhere else through creation of more rules and heavier enforcement.

This category of boondocker is more that of a squatter, of people trying to survive a bad economy, rather than someone who's there for solitude and nature.

At the time of this writing, squatters have become a problem in many areas near cities with nearby public lands, places like Boulder, Colorado and Flagstaff, Arizona, with subsequent arrests and tickets. Some squatters are drug users or have mental-health problems, some are people down on their luck, while some are living that life by choice as they don't want to plug into the system and work at jobs they hate.

Not all, but many of these people tend to be irresponsible when it comes to camp etiquette and pollution. This leads to problems with the locals, and rightfully so, as who wants to see their nearby public lands trashed?

The Rules

Your best bet as a boondocker is to simply stay away from such areas and to not look or act like a squatter. Your camp should be tidy and clean, and it's imperative you follow the rules, which are there to protect the land.

If you're following the rules and are polite and considerate to law enforcement, your odds of having problems are zero. Most rangers are in up to their necks trying to do a job that's understaffed and unappreciated and will respond in like to good treatment.

There is simply no reason to see a ranger as an adversary unless you're trying to break the rules, as they are there to help ensure that your stay is safe and pleasant by kicking out those who break the rules and create an unpleasant environment by leaving trash and making noise and abusing the land.

Keep in mind that when you get lost or have an accident, it's these same rangers who will be there to help you. But it's more common than not to never see a ranger, as land-management districts are large and tend to be understaffed.

As a camp host in a popular area in Utah, I've gotten to know many rangers, and theirs is pretty much a thankless job. There will always be those who abuse power, but I have yet to meet a ranger that wasn't competent and polite, as long as you returned the consideration and respect. It's a tough job, one I wouldn't want, with a high burnout rate. I know one ranger who had to take permanent medical leave for PTSD.

But back to the rules. Most public lands allow what's called "dispersed camping," which means you can camp anywhere that a camp spot already exists or where you won't be damaging anything.

In other words, if you're in the desert and there's no vegetation, you can camp anywhere, as long as you leave no trace. If you're in an area where camp spots have already been created by campers (such as fire rings in a national forest), you can camp there. You should always leave a camp spot like you found it, if not better, and in this case, better means cleaner and less trodden.

Creating a new camp spot is generally frowned upon in all districts, and many places with heavy use often no longer allow dispersed camping, but require you to stay in campgrounds. This is usually the legacy of overuse and abuse.

Of course, national parks and monuments always require that you stay in campgrounds, and boondocking is never allowed there. Wilderness areas usually allow boondocking, but you can't use a motorized vehicle to get there, but must hike in or ride horseback.

In general, the rules for dispersed camping are:

• Pick a site at least one-quarter mile from the nearest paved road or developed campground (this is typically more a forest service rule than for the BLM, but be aware that some districts do the opposite and say you must stay within 100 feet of a main road).

• Use an existing campsite if possible and avoid crushing vegetation.

• Stay at least 100 feet away from water sources so as to reduce pollution and impact on animals who depend on the water.

• Reduce your footprint as much as possible physically and visually, so others aren't as likely to see you or your camp.

• Do not disturb the soil in any way (no trenches, leveling holes, etc.).

• Motorized vehicles must stay on existing roads, and you shouldn't make camp any further from the road than necessary.

• Stay out of historical or archaeological sites, as well as areas where animals or birds migrate, have their young, or must cross to get to water or feed, including near stock tanks.

• Don't leave trash out, as it can blow away and/or attract wildlife. Clean up your camp when you leave;

• Keep a quiet camp.

• After 14 days, you must move camp to another location, usually a minimum of 25 miles away and for at least 28 days before returning to the first camp.

• Campfires may or may not be allowed, but in no case can you cut wood unless it's explicitly stated as being legal (rare), and you must remove all traces of the fire and/or fire ring unless the ring was previously there. Some areas will allow you to collect deadwood. Never leave a fire unattended and be sure it's completely out before leaving camp. Some areas require a free permit for a campfire (e.g., most of California and Nevada). Some areas require you have a shovel handy if building a fire.

• If you pass through a gate, leave it as you found it (whether open or closed). Many areas have ranchers running cattle on permits and they will leave the gates as they want them to be.

In addition, the BLM has what are called LTVAs (Long Term Visitor Areas), primarily in Arizona and California. These areas have their own rules and fees and are often open to continuous camping for several months at a time, providing you have a permit.

Finding Good Boondocking Spots

First, there are several questions one should ask for any site, which are:

• Can I easily turn around and park so I can quickly exit if need be (fire, floods, other threats)?

• Can I park so I can see if anyone is coming into my camp?

• Is there more than one way into my camp in case I need an alternate route out? (This requisite is typically harder to fill.)

• Am I clear of possible falling timber, flashflood danger, and danger from fast-moving fires? How about exposure to lightning strikes (as on ridges, etc.)?

• Where will the sun hit me at different times of the day (especially important if you have solar or are trying to manage heat/cold via window placement, as well as trying to put your awning in the best place)?

• Which direction will the wind typically come from (usually west to east, but not always, as the wind usually reverses direction as a storm passes through)? You'll want to orient your rig accordingly.

• Are there campers nearby, or places where it's probable that weekend campers will park? Am I planning on camping in a place that's going to be popular on weekends and/or holidays?

Finding places to boondock can be partially dependent on the type of rig you have. If you have a big rig with little clearance, you're going to need to be much more methodical than if you have a 4x4 pickup camper that can go almost anywhere. Having a smaller rig gives you much more flexibility, as you can simply drive around until you find a suitable place without doing much, if any, preplanning. This is how I prefer to travel, but I realize I pay for it in comfort, as the smaller rig has less space and fewer amenities.

Probably the most common way to find a spot is to get out the maps. You can purchase hardcopies of maps or download them from the internet. The two most popular printed book sets are DeLorme and Benchmark, which have books for each state. I prefer DeLorme, and some swear by Benchmark, though the newer DeLorme books don't have the level of detail they once had for backroads. Look for the editions from the 1990s, if possible. And don't forget to get regional maps from the local BLM or forest service offices, as they will have much more detail.

Some get out the maps and study them long before picking a destination to see what's easiest to get to, then select their next campsite in that general area. They will sometimes write down or program GPS coordinates into their units and then head out.

I prefer to simply drive around on the backroads until I find a good spot, but when I'm pulling a trailer, I'm much more prone to planning things out. I like Google Earth and have spent many hours using it to study landscapes, determining what roads go where and what looks like a good area for camping.

To me, driving the old logging roads and back roads is part of the fun, but if I were in a big Class A or even a Class C motorhome, I wouldn't be so fearless, though some carry bicycles and will use them to scout out places (or use their toad, i.e., towed vehicle, if they have one).

If I'm unsure of an area or I arrive late at night, I'll sometimes camp in a parking lot for the night, then spend the next day exploring until I find a good spot. If I'm pulling a trailer, I'll sometimes stay in a campground (usually a state one, as I avoid private campgrounds because of their endless rules, close quarters, and high costs). I unhook my trailer and go exploring until I find a good boondocking site, then relocate the trailer.

When using maps to determine possible sites, look for spur roads, as they are often not well-used. These are usually older roads on the map with a letter after the number, and some even have more letters, which indicates they're even older and less likely to be used, such as FR222, which leads to FR222B, and then to FR222B1.

Some boondockers keep notebooks with detailed information about where they camped so they can come back in the future without having to try to recall where they were. After you camp so many places and days, things can get a little mixed up. They'll put in GPS coordinates with other information such as road conditions, how far back in it is, and the views and wildlife, sometimes even adding photos.

Whatever you do, unless you're in a pickup camper, don't just take off on a road and hope for the best. Most boondockers with trailers and bigger rigs have at least one or two horror stories. My own story has to do with the road literally ending in a place where it took me an hour to turn around, even though I was only pulling a small 17-foot trailer, and I was lucky to be able to do that. It led to my selling the trailer and buying a pickup with a camper. I read one story about a guy who had to back his trailer up for a number of miles, as he hadn't checked out the camp spot beforehand and was pulling a large trailer and couldn't turn around.

Another valuable resource is the blogs of other boondockers, though this can easily lead down a number of rabbit holes. But one can keep a list of places you might like to camp someday while reading these blogs, then refer back to the list when in that area. Only problem with this is that others will be doing the same thing. And if you're a blogger, if you like to share your camp spots on the internet, be prepared to share them in real life when you return.

It used to be you could tell others about a campsite and the odds would be good you would still never find anyone in it when you returned, but the internet now makes this information accessible to anyone, and there are more and more campers every year. One popular blogger has made herself unwanted in many camps by afterwards telling everyone where her camps are.

One thing you should be aware of is the elevation of the area you're thinking about camping in, as this will affect the temperatures. If it's summer, lower elevations will be hotter, but in the winter, this is what you want. You can also check weather statistics to get an idea of temperatures and whether or not a spot is windy, though microcosms will also affect this. Online resources are good for this, sites such as Wunderground.com and Weather.com.

And don't forget, when on your way to finding a boondock site, there are lots of free places one can stay temporarily. A brief survey by Truck Camper Magazine of where boondockers had stayed overnight included construction sites, hospitals, hotel parking lots, marinas, behind police stations, at trailheads, on side streets, empty lots filled with weeds, county courthouses, Walmarts, next to a B&B, Elk's Clubs (you must be a member), dirt roads off the highway, convention centers, grocery store and car repair lots, rest areas, Cracker Barrels, wildlife refuges, municipal parks and fairgrounds, truck stops, malls, movie theater lots, industrial areas, and beaches.

Sometimes it's better to ask permission, but other times it's better to ask forgiveness, as the odds are that no one will care.

The upshot is that there are many many places you can camp, but sometimes you have to do your research to find them, unless you're prepared to just drive around, which to me is the fun way. But if you have a large rig, it may get you in trouble, and it's probably wise to plan ahead when looking for a camp spot.

What Will it Cost?

Boondocking can be a great way to save money, assuming you actually do spend most of your time off the grid. But the more you drive around, the more it will cost, both in gas and in vehicle maintenance.

One can live on very little if they're frugal and already have their rig paid for. I know boondockers who live on $500/month, but I can honestly say I can't imagine doing it myself. Many of them are van-dwellers living on Social Security and who stay in one spot as long as possible before moving. It is possible, however, to do more and spend less and still have a healthy, active lifestyle.

One full-time boondocker I met while in Arizona lived in a small 13-foot vintage trailer, and she had the interior fixed up as cute and comfortable as could be. She had a small terrier with her, and the trailer actually seemed fine for the two of them.

She was retired and rotated between Arizona and New Mexico, making jewelry that she sold, though she shared with me that she didn't make much from it. She said her total monthly income averaged around $700. But the bottom line was that she seemed happy.

Another boondocker I met lived in an old pickup camper. He also was retired and had been a handyman all his life. He lived on Social Security of $500/month, and went to Montana for the summer and Arizona for the winter, doing the occasional handyman job to supplement his income. He, too, seemed content and had lots of great stories to tell.

Some boondock because they want to be in nature and away from the stress that can come with being around people, but others boondock from necessity. RVing can be cheap or expensive, depending on how you do it. I've read blogs of boondockers who have more invested in their rigs than many houses cost. (The Earthroamer currently sells for over $250,000.) And then there are those who barely get by.

But it's been my experience that most boondockers do it primarily to enjoy nature, and saving money is a nice side benefit. And those who boondock on their vacations are often families who don't want to be crammed in with other campers in parks or campgrounds.

The cost of staying in a campground is rapidly increasing, whether it be private or federal. In general, most private campgrounds (places like KOA) will cost about one-half of a mid-level motel. Some boondockers like to stay in a motel once in awhile to shower, do laundry, resupply, etc. and can afford it, since they boondock the rest of the time.

Some states have annual camping passes that make the cost of staying in state parks much more affordable. For example, New Mexico has an annual state park permit for around $200, a bit more for non-residents. This lets you stay in any New Mexico state park for free or at a discount, if you choose to have hookups. Utah and Montana both have annual passes that will give you discounts at any of their state parks.

And don't forget senior discounts if you're over 62. Some places are really cheap with a discount, often as low as $5/night.

Some boondockers will get jobs as camp hosts, which provides a stable place to live for the duration of their hosting. Camp host jobs vary as much as any other job, depending on the place, type of campground, and what's expected. Some pay nothing, giving you a site in return for your work. Be wary of these types of jobs if they're in private campgrounds, as they can be very exploitative, and you soon come to realize you're paying a fortune in your time and energy for that "free" campsite. Always compare what a site like that would cost if you weren't working for them and how many hours you're working to get it for "free."

I prefer to camp host at federal or state campgrounds, as the rules are predetermined and you're generally not at the mercy of a campground owner who may try to exploit you.

Federal and state campgrounds (BLM, Forest Service, Army Corp of Engineers) are very up-front about what they expect and what you get in return. Many of them will pay a small stipend, which may not be much (generally $10 to $25/day), but to a frugal boondocker, it adds up. In addition, some will provide solar panels for your use while there.

The website volunteer.gov has listings for what's available in each state at the federal level, and each state will have similar listings for their state campgrounds. Some popular areas are difficult to get host positions with, and others can be had at the last minute. I've noticed that Alaska seems to always be wanting camp hosts, and some agencies there (BLM and FS) pay a pretty good stipend. However, getting there will take time and money unless you're already there.

There's a lot of internet information about how to make a living while RVing, and be aware that some of the paid subscription services are simply trying to sell you information that's free if you're willing to do some research. Pick an area in which you would like to boondock, then start searching for camp host positions, gate guarding jobs, etc. But in all honesty, most of these will take you from the realm of pure boondocking to more of a dry camping experience, as you won't be out in the boonies when you're camp hosting, even though you may still be in a pretty nice place.

In general, though, boondocking is probably one of the cheapest ways one can live, with the bonus of being in the most beautiful and quietest places.

Taking Pets Along

Having a pet can really make the difference when one is boondocking, especially when alone. Pets are good company, and dogs especially will help give you peace of mind, as they make excellent early-alarm systems, though not without the occasional false alarm. Dogs will typically alert you to anything in camp, whether it be a squirrel or a ranger.

Pets can also be very entertaining, and their need for exercise will help ensure you're getting yours, too. And taking care of an animal and being tuned in with them is very rewarding. I cover a lot of pet information in my book, "RVing with Pets," especially about RVing with cats.

Dogs are descendants of wolves, and recent research indicates that, instead of us domesticating the wolves, they domesticated themselves by hanging around our trash piles and slowly working their way into our lives, serving to help protect us in exchange for food. And like wolves, dogs are very happy when roaming. This doesn't mean you should let them run free, but rather, it means that they're well-adapted to the nomadic life.

As most dog owners already know, dogs are generally eager to please. They are the perfect travel companions, and are easy to deal with, as long as their basic needs are met, which includes a need for security, affection, and companionship.

Cats also can make good travel companions, but they're much more likely to disappear if they get the chance, as they're stealth hunters. Even a well-fed cat will roam, checking out the terrain, just in case famine were to suddenly hit.

This tendency to wander makes cats much more difficult to camp with, as they must always be restrained. Some dogs are the same way, especially the hound breeds, but most dogs aren't as sneaky about finding ways to get out. There are, of course, exceptions to this, but having boondocked with both cats and dogs, I find it easier to camp with dogs. Also a component of this is the ever-present litter box. If you have a large rig or can open a cargo door into an area for the box, it makes life easier.

I use a cat tent to let my cats be outside and get fresh air, as well as having a large metal cage. This not only keeps them around, but it protects them from stray dogs and predators. My dogs are good camp dogs and won't run, but if I'm in a campground (rare), I'll tie them to a tie-out stake for the thirty seconds they want to be out before wanting back in again (they think they always need to be with me). Of course, if I'm outside, they love being out.

Cats do have their benefits while camping, one being that they're quiet and don't bark and also sleep a lot. So, on second thought, in some ways cats are easier than dogs. I have both, thereby maximizing the trouble—and rewards. And having cats sure makes for a good way to meet people, as they see them in their cage and come over to see what it's all about, as most people don't camp with cats, though this is changing.

There are a few things you must do before taking your pets boondocking. Having some kind of ID is not optional, for if your pet gets out and is lost, it's the only way you'll ever see them again. Always put your phone number, email, and name on the tag. Some people buy extra large tags and also put things like "On the road, trailer is a white Scamp, plates CO234." I also write my phone number on the collar in black marker in case they lose their tags.

I have all my pets microchipped, as the first thing a vet or animal service officer will do when finding a lost pet is to scan them for a chip. This will link to a service with your phone number, and they can call you. Micro-chipping is an easy and fairly painless procedure that doesn't cost much (usually under $50/pet).

Create a hardcopy file on each pet with their name and vaccination history (especially rabies), as well as any medicines they may take. Keep this in your rig in case something happens to you and someone else needs to take care of them. In addition, some will create a digital file with copies of their rabies certificates and medical records.

Such files, whether hardcopy or digital, will also come in handy if you're on the road and need to take your pet to a vet. If you decide to travel to Canada or Mexico, you'll find this information invaluable.

Also, have a good photo of each of your pets in case you need to post a lost flyer, though this should never happen if you're careful, though I did read about an RVer in a motorhome in Alaska who was in an accident and her cat was lost. It was found months later because she had posted photos of it everywhere and someone recognized it.

Always have a sign inside your rig stating that you have animals and how many of each, along with your phone number and a backup number in case you're somehow incapacitated or out of range. Some people will hide a key nearby so someone can get into the rig if there's an emergency.

It's best to never leave your pets in your rig, but if you do have to go somewhere, always put a note on your vehicle's dash or in an obvious place that states you have pets and where they can be found.

I recently read a harrowing story about a fellow who boondocks full time and ended up in the ER of the local hospital with a sudden onset life-threatening condition. He was flown to a larger city while unconscious, so no one even knew he'd left his two dogs in his trailer in a very remote location.

It all worked out OK, but only because a close friend knew he had dogs, but it was very difficult for them to figure out where he was camped, which they did, but only by trial and error. This kind of situation is not as likely to happen if you're not camping solo.

Always have a pet emergency kit that includes:

• Tweezers for removing ticks, stickers, cactus, etc.

• Disinfectant such as Betadine

• Gauze and tape (to wrap injuries)

• Epsom salts (for swelling)

• Hydrogen peroxide (to induce vomiting, if needed)

• Benadryl (for allergic reactions or stings)

• Digital thermometer

See the Chapter 18 on helpful things to take for more detail on an emergency pet kit.

It goes without saying you should have pet carriers handy for your cats and smaller dogs, kept in a place easily accessed in an emergency.

If you need emergency pet care, you can always do an internet search to see who is nearby, assuming you have the internet. If you have to, call a friend and have them Google it. As for regular pet care, sites like Trip Advisor are great for checking out nearby vets. If there's a problem, it's likely to be mentioned. Local Humane Societies and shelters can also recommend good vets.

When camping with pets, always leave your camp better than you found it and clean up after them. Wild animals never pollute their own bedding places or dens.

My dogs stay in camp, but I also have small LED lights that attach to their collars that I use if they're out after dark. These little clip-on lights are available in places like Petco. It's nice even when I'm just sitting around a campfire to be able to see exactly where they are.

My dogs stay in camp and never chase wildlife (they're working dogs and are very obedient), but if you have a dog that likes to wander or chase, please restrain them, as there's nothing worse than losing a dog in the backcountry and you can also be fined for harassing wildlife. You can buy portable panels and create a small fenced area near your rig for your dog or you can also buy 15 or 20 foot leads and tie them.

In general, boondocking with pets makes everything much more fun, as well as safer and more enjoyable, especially if you're a solo camper. And if you rescue a pet from an animal shelter, you'll have a lifelong loyal friend.

Basic Survival

What to Eat?

What to eat when you're boondocking isn't going to be that much different from what you would eat at home, though you may have fewer fresh items and you probably won't be doing much, if any, baking.

You may find that you gravitate towards making things that are easier to cook and take fewer pans, as you'll have to wash everything later. Sometimes it's just easier to run into town, wherever town may be, and get something like a quesadilla at the quesadilla wagon.

If you have a refrigerator, you can stay out longer and have a wider variety of foods, including salads and items that are harder to keep fresh in a cooler. I tend to use a cooler instead of the refrigerator, and coolers do not keep things good for nearly as long, especially if you're not near town where you can get ice.

I'll open my cooler, and see things that are going bad, and since I'm a little bit picky but also hate to waste food, I give it to my dogs, who eat quite well. Since I'm not much of a cook, I tend to buy enough fresh stuff, such as for making salads, for a few days, then I'll eat things like peanut butter and jelly, and eventually will go into town and get something tasty.

In that sense, I'm not the most hard-core of boondock-ers, as I'll go into town every few days, and I tend not to camp more than 20 miles out. I do know people who will go weeks before going into town and camp hours and hours away from the nearest store, going only out of necessity.

I think most boondockers are somewhere in the middle, going into town maybe once a week to get rid of trash and get fresh groceries, or maybe even more often.

But it's an entirely individual matter, and I know one boondocker who thinks nothing of driving 60 miles to get a sandwich, though I think it's actually an excuse to go so-cialize.

One of the problems in camping solo is that you do get tired of the same food after awhile. You can make a deli-cious pizza, then store the individual slices, eating on it for several days, but you then get really tired of pizza.

I used to do a lot of tent camping, and I was such a minimalist that I wouldn't even take a cooler. Basically, my diet consisted of granola and dried fruits, and for protein, I would eat an occasional can of tuna or chicken. Fortunately, I don't care for meat, which makes storage easier. I also don't tend to consume many dairy products, using only a little milk in my daily coffee.

There are some campers who have barbecues and stock their refrigerators and whip up very tasty meals every day, seldom going into town to eat out. In a way, I envy their industriousness.

I generally do pretty well with my small repertoire of edibles, but I have noticed that when a big storm is brew-ing, when it's gray and cloudy and dreary and bleak, I tend to crave comfort foods.

There are lots of camping cookbooks, and about the only thing I've ever gotten into is foil cooking, which is easy, but requires a fire. After the fire has burned down into hot coals, you can put meat and/or vegetables wrapped in foil into the coals, letting them cook for as long as necessary. You can cook anything that also cooks well in an oven, except for baked goods, of course.

Some are really into Dutch-oven cooking, and stir-fry type meals are also popular. You can also purchase 12 volt frying pans, toasters, and even small ovens. Dutch-oven cooking is an art that takes a lot of time, but the resulting meals are usually delicious and varied, including things like biscuits and cakes and cobblers, which are hard to make otherwise.

For me, the real secret to happy boondocking is to plan ahead and stock up for all occasions, but you shouldn't have to suffer and not enjoy good food, even if it means going into town occasionally.

And the truth about camping is that you can eat about anything you would eat at home, though sometimes it just takes a little more trouble.

Water

The first thing to know about water is your own daily consumption, plus that of your pets, if you have any. Once you know how much you need, you can plan accordingly.

I generally average about one to two gallons a day for myself, which includes washing dishes, spit baths, etc. I add another gallon or two for my dogs, depending on how hot it is.

You can reduce your own water consumption in a variety of ways. First, camp somewhere that's not too warm, especially if you do a lot of hiking. Camping in the heat will guarantee your consumption goes up, as you want to drink plenty of water when it's hot.

Another good way to reduce water use is to use just one drop of soap when washing your dishes, which does the job and requires less rinsing. Or don't even use soap—if you cook with little to no meat or cheeses, your dishes will generally clean up well with just a little water.

A lot of boondockers start out using plastic and paper dishes and silver, but they soon realize they're trading lower water usage for more trash, plus they're being less environmentally aware. And, the cost of such does add up over time.

Water is one of the most common ways that boondockers get sick, and many don't even realize it. We assume that if water comes from a spigot, it's potable, but even if that's the case, it may still have bacteria or microbes that you're not used to and will give you the same effects as having a mild case of food poisoning.

If you have a trailer or rig with an on-board water tank, you should rinse and sterilize it occasionally with bleach to prevent growth in the tank. I prefer to carry my water in Reliance water containers, which are quick to fill, easy to carry, and equally easy to rinse out and clean. Not keeping your water containers clean is a good way to make yourself sick.

If you're in an area where there are streams, you may want to filter your water. I would not recommend filtering from a pond or a slow river, and if you've ever had giardia, you'll understand my reluctance to use anything but treated water. My brother had it and almost died. He got it from a stream in Oregon—he'd been told it was safe by a fellow hiker, though as a seasoned hiker he knew he was taking a risk.

Giardia is also called "beaver fever" and can be acquired any place where animals drink from that water, which is pretty much everywhere. A good filter will remove the bacteria, but with all the other pollutants in today's streams, you're taking a chance on other bad things being in your water.

Try to get your water from municipal sources, and be sure your hose is also cleaned periodically with bleach, as it can also be a source of bacteria. You can buy bottled water, but it gets expensive and there's really no guarantee that the water's any better than that of the nearest town.

Dealing with Trash

Of all the things that you'll have to deal with while boondocking, trash and water seem to be the most persistent, and trash can be even harder than water to deal with.

With water, you can fill your tank or jugs and know you'll be good for x number of days, depending on how much capacity you have, but trash comes and goes (mostly comes), and dealing responsibly with trash in the backcountry isn't necessarily an easy task.

The best way to deal with trash is to not have any to start with. Of course, this is hard to do, but I found that one thing that really helps is to grocery shop in the bulk section. Not only is this usually cheaper, but you don't generate as much trash, as things are not packaged.

When I go to the grocery store, the first thing I do after I load the groceries into my rig is to go through everything and try to get rid of as much packaging as possible. For example, if you buy a box of crackers, the crackers are in another package inside, and all the box does is protect them. So, I get rid of the box and put the crackers in a safe place. Another example might be cookies. I'll take them from the original package and put them into little plastic sandwich baggies, kind of as a daily ration, and then get rid of the box or package that they came in.

After I go through the groceries, I take all the packaging and recycle as much of it as possible, then throw the rest away while I'm still in town. But some things you can't dispose of until after you've used the product, so you will always have trash. Cans are a good example of this.

It also helps to not buy things you really don't need. One example of this might be baby wipes. A lot of RVers think they need baby wipes to stay clean, but all you need is water. You can burn things like baby wipes, but I always am concerned about anything with chemicals in it and would not want to stand downwind of the fire. Things with lots of chemicals belong in the landfill. So, one thing I do is try not to buy things that have a lot of chemicals in them.

You'll find that after you boondock for awhile, your sense of smell becomes heightened. The best scent of all is the scent of fresh air and pine trees or sagebrush, and after awhile, you may find yourself sniffling when you walk down the supermarket aisle that has all the detergents and scented house-cleaning products.

Once you get away from all the scented products, you begin to realize how scent is used to manipulate you into buying things. Studies have shown that various scents have strong associations and can actually create endorphins. Once you're free from such things you become much more aware of them when you're around them and they can become very irritating. When you live in a natural environment, things that aren't so natural become much more noticeable.

While camping, you can bag your trash, and it's handy to have something to further contain it to keep animals and insects out. For example, I have a big round tub with handles on it that's about three feet in diameter, and this is where I store my trash bags.

At night, I put this tub inside my vehicle, because I don't want to get up in the morning and have to pick up trash. If you have anything that critters can get into, they will. And this is even more critical when camping in bear country.

Once this tub gets full, I then have to decide whether or not it's time to make a trash run and go to the nearest town. This can typically be about once a week, if I'm careful to not start out with much trash.

Some people will burn their trash, but you should have a fire pit and be careful about when you choose to burn, following the same rules you would if you were burning wood. Be sure that campfires are legal where you're at.

It's also important to not burn things like plastic, as they put out noxious odors and you can end up poisoning yourself, not to mention what you leave behind.

Some think it's okay to throw bottles and cans in the fire pit and "burn" them, leaving them behind with the ashes.

This is quite simply nothing less then leaving your trash behind.

Many popular camp spots have had fire rings built by previous campers, and quite often when you arrive, they need to be cleaned out. Sometimes it's just ashes, but other times it's just plain trash. It's good camping etiquette to always leave a clean camp, but many don't. Those who don't are contributing to places being closed to campers.

A lot of people will burn their cardboard and paper products, but it really is better to take them to the recycle place. Camping makes you realize how much trash we really do generate.

Getting rid of your trash might be a problem or it might not. For example, in the little town of Green River, Utah there are literally trash dumpsters about every block for public use. The town has no trash on its streets because it makes it so easy to throw trash away. It's a good community service and lets tourists and backcountry campers know they're welcome.

Just down the road only 50 miles is the town of Moab, which is an outdoor recreation paradise. It's been discovered and is full of kitschy restaurants and shops, unlike Green River, which is just a basic small town. However, Moab has nowhere to get rid of trash—literally nowhere. The dumpsters are all carefully locked and watched over by the businesses they belong to, and if you try to throw your trash in them, you're made to feel like a common criminal.

So what do you do with your trash when you're in a town like Moab? Well, seasoned campers will put their trash into small grocery bags instead of trashcan-sized bags, making it easy to stuff them into gas station or grocery-store trash cans.

I've watched in amazement as people will fill an entire gas-station trashcan with small grocery-store bags, thereby getting rid of all their trash.

Like the poor, trash will always be with us. And the one recurring problem you will always have while boondocking is getting rid of your trash.

Staying Clean

I think the one thing that bothers me most when boondocking is not being able to take a morning shower—that is, until after a few days, when it no longer bothers me.

I've adapted and lowered my standards, which isn't to say I like being dirty, but that I've adopted different ways of making sure I'm clean. Admittedly, none are as good or as effective as a nice long hot shower, but then, it's worth the price to be out in some of the most beautiful places on Earth.

You actually can shower when boondocking, and a number of devices (such as a propane shower heater) can be purchased to make it more efficient, but they all take water, which is a precious commodity unless you're camped by a lake or stream, then you can shower at will.

One method is the solar-shower bag, a bladder that typically holds about five gallons of water and that you fill and set in the sun, resulting in hot water after a few hours. These are actually very effective, but are hard to use, as you have to hang them from a tree or something stout to use them. Shower enclosures are handy for this, but to me are just one more piece of equipment one has to pack and unpack and setup as needed. I simply wait until it's dark and no one can see me to shower.

You can also purchase portable hot-water heaters that run on propane, which many swear by, but which tend to be rather expensive (some are over $200). For me, simply heating water on the stove and mixing it with cold water works fine. I can shower with two gallons, which includes washing my medium-length hair. Always use biodegradable soaps.

Spit baths are a necessity when boondocking, which simply means washing up with a washcloth, which is quick and easy. I'll do this for a couple of days, then take a good shower.

If I'm near a town, I've found that recreation centers often have showers for a few dollars, especially if they have a swimming pool. These are the best, much better than taking a shower at a state park or private RV park, where they often charge you by the minute. Some state parks require you to pay a night's camp fee just for a shower (Green River State Park in Utah is one example). Montana state parks charge by the minute.

Keeping your clothes clean usually requires going to a laundromat, though some will hand-wash their clothes. I have yet to meet anyone who likes them, but some are much better than others. A good laundromat is not noisy or busy, is clean, cheap, and has internet. It's truly rare to find all these things in one place, but you can generally beat the crowds by doing your laundry on weekday mornings. Stay away on weekends, as that's when the working folks do theirs.

Dealing with Body Wastes

Like water, this can be a real limiting factor in how long you can stay out. How you deal with it is going to largely depend on what kind of rig you have. If your rig has a bathroom and therefore has holding tanks, your limit is how long you can go before the tanks are full. When the tanks are full, it's time to go find a dump station.

Your rig will have two waste-water tanks—one will be a gray water tank which is where everything that goes through your sink ends up, and the other will be a black water tank, which holds the waste from your toilet. Of course, you will also have a third tank, which is used for your drinking water.

When you dump your tanks, you always dump the black water tank first and then the gray water tank, using the gray water to flush out the black water and pipes. Usually, the bigger the trailer, the bigger the tanks, and the bigger your tanks, the longer you can boondock.

But there's also the limiting factor of having a large rig, which means you quite often can't get into the backcountry like you would like. This is why you see the big Class A diesel-pusher type rigs in RV parks. And so you have to weigh what your needs and wants are against which type of rig you buy or already have.

The other end of the spectrum is someone camping in their car and/or using a tent. Close to this extreme is living in a pickup with a shell or canopy on it, or in a van. These people have completely different issues to deal with then someone in a big RV that has a bathroom with holding tanks.

Hauling water is also rig dependent. Someone in a big Class A can haul up to 100 gallons of water whereas a small 17-foot trailer will typically have a 21-gallon water tank, with a 27-gallon gray-water tank and a 20 gallon black-water tank.

When you winter boondock in cold country, you won't be able to use your tanks unless you have some way of heating them. A four-season rig will come with extra insulation and heated tanks (typically using heat strips), which often means they're heated only if you have an electrical hookup.

These include the Bigfoot and the Escape trailers, both which were originally made in Canada. Bigfoot is now made in the United States, but the Escape is still made in British Columbia. Both trailers are well-known for their insulation and warmth in the winter. And keep in mind that such insulation will also keep you cooler in the summer, as well as making the interior quieter.

There are tricks you can utilize to use your tanks in the winter, such as putting antifreeze in them, but you still risk them freezing if it gets very cold. Some simply winterize their rigs and use them as hard-walled tents having very nice heaters.

I now use a porta potty, which means not having to worry about it freezing and also increasing my boondocking time before I have to go back to town to dump tanks. Porta parties are great because they're portable, easy to dump, will keep you going for a week or more, don't need chemicals (although you can use them), and are easy to stick in a corner.

But how you deal with your own wastes all depends on you and what you want to do—the size of the rig you want to haul around, how long you want to be able to stay out, and things like that.

Dealing with and emptying gray and black water tanks is a science all unto itself. There are many techniques for emptying tanks without making a big mess, and special tools that go with that, and also chemicals that you must use. Often, when one enters a rig with a black tank, you instantly know because of the chemical smell.

This all adds up to a number of people who go for simplicity and refuse to use gray and black water tanks at all. Be aware that some areas require you to have some sort of toilet, and if a ranger comes around, they may very well ask you to prove that you have the proper facilities. Once again, this has evolved because of people abusing the wilderness and leaving trash and waste wherever they happen to be.

Some boondockers have installed composting toilets in their rigs with good success, although these can be expensive ($1,000 and up). But they certainly solve the problem of having tanks to dump.

So, how do people deal with waste when they're out boondocking and don't have toilets in their rigs? Some boondockers like to dig cat holes. To use the cat hole method, you go as far away from camp as possible, dig a hole at least six inches deep, go potty, bury it, and pack out or burn your toilet paper.

The cat hole method is, in my opinion, one that should be abandoned. I've camped where people have used this method, and it can quickly render a very nice camp spot uninhabitable. And in some climates, such as the desert southwest, it takes years for things to disintegrate, and the cat hole method becomes disgusting.

One of the main problems is that people don't dig their holes deep enough, and there are a number of wild animals that will dig up scat and eat it, such as the coyote, and human manure can make an animal very sick because of all the bacteria. The cat hole method has led to many areas in the West being shut down to campers.

A very popular method among van-dwellers is to use a bucket with a toilet seat on it. You line the bucket with plastic trash bags and tie them up when you're finished, placing them in the trash, or in another bucket with a lid on it. The problem with this is that you go through a lot of plastic bags, and they really become smelly after a while. You really want to dump your trash every day or two when you're using this method, which can be hard to do. Some people will line the bucket with cat litter or sawdust and just use the bucket until it's full.

So, these are the main methods of dealing with waste when boondocking. Whichever method you decide on, please haul out your waste. There's nothing nicer than driving into a camp spot and thinking you're the first one to ever camp there because the previous campers left it so clean.

Bad Weather

Full-time Boondockers and RVers typically have routes that they generally follow according to the weather and time of the season, going south in the winter and north in the summer.

No matter where you camp, it's a good idea to keep an eye on the weather. And in this vein, probably the best purchase you can make is a weather radio, as mentioned earlier.

I personally prefer the little wind-up weather radios that have a little solar panel on them and that one can also wind up. These typically will have AM and FM stations, as well as weather radio frequencies which will pick up the nearest weather station from NOAA. It goes without speaking that the quality of the speaker on these is poor enough you won't want to listen to music on it unless you're desperate. (I will admit that sometimes I listen to my weather radio just to hear the sound of another human voice, even though it's synthesized.)

If you're camped way out in the back country, it's imperative that you keep an eye on the weather, especially if you're out where the roads become impassible when wet. Much of the west has bentonite clay, which is a combination of clay and ash from long–ago volcanic eruptions. Bentonite clay has also been called "death mud" by those who have tried to drive it when wet. It's much like trying to steer a toboggan. Even having a four-wheel drive vehicle won't save you from death mud. Many great campfire stories revolve around narrow escapes from such.

Another thing one must be aware of, particularly in slickrock country, is the potential for flash flooding. In these areas, rain does not necessarily slowly percolate into the soil, but instead runs off, going downhill into the nearest drainages, creating rivulets that merge into small streams that merge into raging rivers.

And sometimes a raging river can appear where one would never expect it and a dry arroyo can become an impassable threat. This is one good reason to never camp in a low area or stream bed. And be aware that flashflooding can also affect you even if you're miles away from the water.

For example, to get to one of my favorite spots in southeast Utah, I have to cross a wide wash. This wash is approximately 60 feet wide, and not long ago, a number of campers were caught on the wrong side of the wash as it turned into a wide raging river after the area got two inches of rain.

Even though they were in no danger, they were prevented from leaving the area until the water receded, which took a good day. And to further complicate matters, sometimes a sandy wash will have pockets of quicksand after it's been flooded which can last for days.

So, it's a good idea to keep an eye on the weather. Sometimes it's prudent to camp closer to town, or even in town, if bad weather's coming in. I recall once actually driving in under someone's empty carport in a little Canadian town when a huge hailstorm suddenly appeared.

It's especially prudent to be aware of incoming winds. If you're camped in a tent, popup trailer, or larger RV, this is particularly important. High winds can really be devastating. I've been known to even park next to a building in town when there were high winds, using it as a windbreak. I would never try to sit out high winds in a tent or pop-up camper.

As a campground host, one of my self-imposed duties was to collect tents that had blown into the outback. I would turn these into the lost and found at our campground, and if no one claimed them, which usually they didn't, they were donated to the local nonprofit thrift store, if still usable. Unfortunately, most of the tents I found had been demolished by the wind.

I recall once trying to console a camper who returned to find his very expensive tent completely gone. The wind had blown it a good half-mile away, over a cliff and into a canyon, where it could only be retrieved by a ten-mile hike.

There are times when civilization has its merits, and high winds is one of those. Motels are well worth their price in some kinds of weather. You can always sleep in your car, assuming it's big enough, but even then, having the wind buffet it back-and-forth usually doesn't make for a good nights sleep.

If you know that high winds are coming, and you don't want to escape into town, there are things you can do to mitigate it. For example, if you're in a trailer, keep it hooked to your vehicle, put the levelers down for extra stability, and face everything into the direction of the storm. Of course, after a storm has come through, the winds will shift, so you may need to move your vehicle again. But usually the highest winds are at the leading edge of the front.

If you're in an area that has large rocks or even some hills that might protect you, move camp to the nearest windbreak. If you're in a tent, you can use your vehicle as a windbreak, and I have even tied my tent to my car when I knew especially high winds were coming in. My car was not big enough to sleep in, and I will say it was a scary experience, trying to sleep in a tent in 60 m.p.h. winds, but I didn't blow away.

Put everything you can inside. Placing things under your vehicle or RV will not keep them from blowing away, nor will putting rocks on them. If the winds are high enough, anything will blow away, and you should act accordingly.

Of course, it goes without saying that if you have an awning, you should roll it up and make sure it's locked in place. The same goes with any kind of portable solar panels, and if you have panels on your roof that tilt, make sure to put them flush with your roof.

I've watched as heavy anti-gravity loungers disappeared into the distance, carried along like leaves. Fortunately, winds like that are not that common.

If you have enough advance notice, remember that you're mobile and can just move, go to a new area and outrun the weather. This is what many RVers do. They watch the internet carefully, and if a big storm is coming in, they will go somewhere else. Being able to ditch bad weather is one of the beauties of living the nomadic life.

If you do decide to sit out the storm, don't forget to cut way back on your electrical usage, as your solar panels probably won't be generating much current. A big storm can last for days, so be prepared, making sure you have enough food and water. These are all things you would have to do in a house also, but when boondocking you don't have as much storage space, so it's more critical to plan ahead. This is a good argument for having the internet, as you can watch the radar and see where the storm is, although a weather radio is generally almost as good.

Climate is a different topic from weather, and dealing with the heat and cold require different strategies that typically involve some form of technology, whether it be a heat source or an air conditioner and the power it takes to run them.

The best way to deal with climate is to go south in the winter and north in the summer, though changing altitude can often have the same effect.

Staying Warm

The beauty of boondocking is that you can follow the seasons and go where it's warm in the winter and cool in the summer, but what about those times when a cold front hits or it gets way too hot for comfort, even though you're at 8,000 feet?

A good rule of thumb is that if it's too warm or cold to stay comfortable, it's time to head somewhere else. But even if you find a place with nice cool days, it's likely you'll have even cooler nights and want something to take off the chill. And vice versa for the heat. No place is ever perfectly comfortable both night and day, and that's why we humans have to wear clothes and invent ways to stay cool and warm.

The most obvious thing to do when it's cold is to put on more clothes, but there's a limit to how warm that will keep you if it's really cold. And when boondocking, you have a limited amount of resources you can use before you're forced back to civilization, so you want to be frugal with your fuel.

The best methods for staying warm combine using energy sources (a heater) with low-tech methods such as managing your rig and having the best clothing and sleeping bags possible (more on this later).

If you like to sit around on cold days in your t-shirt and shorts running the heater at full blast, you may end up having to go many miles for unnecessary propane refills. If you run down your battery, you may have to resort to running a generator, assuming you have one, and this means keeping enough fuel around for that.

Most rigs come with heaters, but not all. I once owned a Casita that didn't have a forced-air furnace, and it made me decide to never again own a rig without one, even though I managed to survive. But if you find a good deal on a rig with no heater, you can always use a Little Buddy or Wave heater, which some prefer to the forced air furnace anyway.

To me, the forced-air furnace is the most pleasant and livable, as well as the safest. You pretty much set the thermostat and that's it. The problem with forced air is that the fan uses a lot of energy and will quickly drain your batteries, as well as being noisy and interfering with TV and radio signals.

Forced-air heaters have even heating and will discharge the combustion gases outside of the trailer, but they can be the source of fire that can quickly inundate your rig. A professional should always do the installation, as it's critical that the return air is nowhere close to the hot-air outlet. If the limit switch fails (usually caused by unnecessary cycling from return air), it can cause a fire. If your fan is running a lot when the actual heater isn't on, the limit switch is cycling, and you should shut your furnace down immediately and have it fixed. It is normal for the fan to run a few minutes after the furnace heater has shut down in order to cool it off.

Another way to heat your rig is to use what are called vent-free propane heaters, such as the infrared radiant types (ceramic and catalytic varieties, which include the Olympian Wave series), and blue-flame heaters.

Vent-free heaters use radiant heat, warming the actual interior surfaces in the rig instead of heating cold air. Vent-free heaters are usually mounted on a wall or sit in a stand and can require plumbing an external propane source into the rig for the heater. These type of heaters generally range from $100 to $400 for cost.

The problem with catalytic heaters is that they can be very dangerous, as they generate carbon monoxide. Every winter, I read of someone who has been killed, sometimes as the result of bad installations or by not keeping an airflow going through their sleeping area (have a window open at least six inches). But people like these types of heaters because they are quiet and don't create interference. They do create higher levels of humidity, however, which can be a problem if everything gets damp, making you feel colder.

It's also a good idea to put some type of cover over your catalytic heater when not using it, even if just a plastic bag, as the orifice is very susceptible to even small amounts of dust. And be sure to check the altitude ratings, a some are not recommended for over 4500 feet.

Another and much more portable type of heater is the Mr. Heater Buddy series, which are portable propane heaters, as well as the Colman Black Cat. These are made for the one-pound propane bottles, though you can buy an adaptor for 10-pound or 25-pound bottles. You can buy long hoses to reach said bottles, as you don't want them inside your rig, as they can be a fire hazard. This means going through a window or even cutting a small hole in your wall to accommodate the hose.

The main problem I have with these types of heaters is that they don't have thermostats and usually just have settings for high or low. Low may not keep you warm enough, and high may run you out of the camper, but you have nothing in between. In addition, the one-pound bottles will only last a few hours if it's under 30 degrees. These types of heaters can be had for under $100, including the adaptor and hose, which makes them popular. Most big-box stores will have these in stock.

Whatever you use, be sure to have a carbon monoxide detector, and always have a window cracked open for fresh air. And one nice thing about heaters that don't have electric blowers is that they will work regardless of whether you have solar or electricity, all you need is propane, and they are quiet.

It's important to never use a cookstove for heating. Any kind of propane stove can kill you, as they all create carbon monoxide, which is odorless and tasteless. With CO, you don't know you're being poisoned until you get very sleepy, and by then you're not likely to be aware enough to recognize the cause.

I was once poisoned with CO while sleeping in an old log cabin in the Colorado Rockies that had an unsafe heating system (unbeknownst to me), and I was lucky to survive. I woke up throwing up from a toxic headache, a symptom of CO poisoning. The fire department came out and tested and evacuated the building.

CO poisoning can also happen when tent camping, so always use a CO detector when using any kind of propane for a heat source, and be sure the batteries in it are good.

Other heat sources include wood or oil burning stoves and diesel hydronic boiler systems, but these are impractical for most people.

Other ways to warm up a space include burning a candle, heating up water, or even running your computer. Some will run their heater until they get good and warm in bed, then turn it off. Good sleeping bags are critical when it's cold. You can also close the bedroom door into your rig and just heat that room. I find that dogs are the best heat source there is, as long as they sleep with you.

Once you have it warm inside, you want to keep it that way, and there are things you can do to help your rig conserve heat.

First, plan ahead. If it's a nice warm day but you know the night will be cold, manage your rig appropriately by closing the windows and curtains while it's still warm.

One handy way to know when the sun will set is to hold your hand up at arm's length to the sun, with your fingers held against one another. Each finger indicates 15 minutes of sun, so four fingers between the bottom of the sun's orb and the horizon means it will set in an hour.

Reflectix bubble insulation is a good inexpensive way to add extra insulation to your windows. Simply buy a roll and cut pieces that will fit into your windows, using templates you've made from paper or cardboard. If you cut the Reflectix a hair larger than the window, it can be easily wedged in for maximum insulation. Don't forget your vents, and having heavy curtains on top of this will add even more insulation.

Keep lots of throw blankets around. I prefer down comforters as wraps for when I'm not ready for bed but want to read. And lots of floor rugs will also help.

And of course, dress appropriately. Sweat pants and tops make great sleeping wear, and when it's really cold, I'll wear warm socks and a felt-lined wool hat. I've camped at temperatures well below zero, which is when I put my down vest on top of my other sleepwear. I've found that flannel hoodies are great also, as the hood helps retain the warm air from your body, circulating it to your head.

Research has shown that cold drinks are actually better for warming your body when it's cold out, as the cold drink causes your capillaries to open up, increasing your blood circulation. And vice versa for when it's hot—drink hot drinks. Counterintuitive, but true.

Other things you can do to help stay warm is to park your rig so the greatest amount of window glass receives the most sun. For example, if you have a large back window, orient your trailer so that window gets the most morning sun, helping warm things up. Be sure to adjust your windows to however you want them before it gets cold at night, as they may freeze in the position you left them in until it warms up the next day.

One of the more serious problems you'll have when it's cold is condensation, especially if it's humid outside. Water vapor absorbs more heat than dry air. Keeping several windows cracked open is good for clearing carbon monoxide, but will also cut down on condensation. Some keep their range vent open.

Several days of rain or high humidity can wreak havoc on a camper or trailer, and it will start feeling damp and moldy. If it's really cold, your rugs and curtains will start freezing to the floor and windows, and you may actually start getting drips and places where the water runs down the walls.

Even if it's really cold, it's imperative that you air your rig out at least once a day for as long as it takes to reduce the moisture. Even if it's raining outside, let some fresh air in.

Don't hang wet things in your rig or cook inside, as this will add even more moisture to the air. Cook outside under a tarp, as you don't want to have your awning out in the cold, as you want the sun heating up your rig.

Some keep cups of dehumidifying crystals in their cupboards and storage areas for humidity control, and don't forget to check under your mattress and cushions, as they may be wet. Use towels to wipe the moisture off the windows and doors each morning.

Orient your rig so it gets the most possible sunlight, staying out from under shade trees and away from rock walls that will block the light. It's best to avoid deep canyons and places that block the sun. And if you don't want your plumbing systems to freeze, it's best to drain them completely and winterize them with antifreeze. If you do choose to use your plumbing, be sure to insulate it, as well as leaving your cupboards open during the night to let heat get to the plumbing.

Make sure your rig doesn't have any leaks. You can also insulate your cupboards, as well as hanging a thick blanket over your door to help keep any drafts out when you open it to go in and out. I have also seen people put clear shower curtains over their windows on the inside to let the sun in but keep drafts out.

If you're keeping your water in jugs, remember that frozen water takes more space, so leave a little air space on top of the jug for expansion, or you'll have a ruptured jug. And you don't want to have to thaw your water to use it, so use larger jugs, which are less likely to freeze. It has to get pretty cold for a seven-gallon container to freeze solid.

In general, the best way to stay warm is to stay in warm country, so try to spend your winters in the southwest at low elevations. There's a reason so many boondockers go to Arizona for the winter—it's warm, dry, and has lots of sunshine. Just be prepared for lots of wind.

Staying Cool

There's a limit to what you can take off when it's hot, a limit either imposed by decency or because there's nothing left to take off (if solo camping). Besides, taking off your clothes invites bug bites and sunburn, neither of which are much fun.

The basic thing to remember is that if the sun is shining, it's heating up anything and everything it shines on, so staying cool means reflecting or shading its rays.

Manage Your Rig

Most boondockers do not use air conditioners, as they don't want to be running their generators all the time, and a generator is the only way you can use an AC, as they take too much power for solar.

One can use 12-volt fans, as long as you have a way to recharge your power source. The most effective of these is the Fantastic Fan, which can be installed in the ceiling of your RV (most come with them factory installed) or you can buy stand-alone ones with a 12 volt pug (be sure you have a 12 volt receptacle if you want to use this). For these, you need solar or a generator.

Fantastic Fans are incredibly effective, and I've had them keep my small trailer comfortable up to about 90 degrees. They basically keep the air flowing, as they have no cooling mechanism. Having two is better, as you can create a good airflow through your trailer, though one is usually sufficient. If you keep a shaded window open and then set the fan to exhaust, it will pull the warmer lighter air in your rig outside.

The hottest time of the day is usually between about four p.m. to seven p.m., and after that, evening breezes will start cooling things off. Of course, just as in staying warm, the best thing for staying cool is to be at a higher altitude, generally above 8,000 feet in the summer.

It's also important to park your rig accordingly, with shade on the west side where the afternoon sun will generate the most heat. If possible, also orient it so you get cross ventilation from any breezes.

Do all you can to prevent the trailer from getting hot in the first place. The more shade you have, the more natural ventilation you'll have available. When you first get up in the morning, open the trailer up—all the windows, vents, and doors—and even if you have to put on a jacket, get as much cool air inside as possible. This will also help cut down condensation.

Once it starts to heat up, close everything up, including your door, which most of us like to keep open when it's nice outside. This will help trap cool air in as long as possible.

Be sure to have your awning out, as it will provide shade for that side of your rig. Tarps are inexpensive and can be used for shading other parts of your camp. You can also use the same Reflectix you cut for your windows to help keep the sun out, fitting it into the windows that get direct sunlight.

Better yet, combine Reflectix with sunscreens that cover your windows outside, keeping the sun from hitting them in the first place. Suncreen material can be purchased at places like Home Depot, isn't expensive, and will reduce solar heat by 70 percent without reducing your interior light.

Other Ways to Stay Cool

Do your outdoors hikes or physically active tasks while it's still cool in the morning, saving the hotter part of the day for sitting in the shade and reading, swimming, or kayaking.

Do all your cooking outside so you don't add to any indoor heat. Set up a camp table outside and keep your stove and coffee/tea items on it. In addition, don't use things indoors that give off heat, such as your computer.

This is one time I'm glad to not use my refrigerator, though ice would be nice, as refrigerators give off heat, even though it's mostly ducted outside. It's also good to eat things that don't require cooking, like salads, chips and salsa, sandwiches, hummus, fruit, etc.

Drink lots of water and cool your body either in a stream or by pouring water over your head, if you have plenty of water. Being hydrated is good for you, and will also help you feel cooler.

One thing that I always do when it's hot is dress in cotton from head to toe. I wear cotton long-sleeved shirts, cotton pants, and a cotton hat, as well as a lightweight neck scarf with an SPF rating.

Like drinking a hot drink to stay cool, this seems counterintuitive, but desert dwellers all over the world have used it effectively for thousands of years. The black feathers on the raven have the same effect, which is to create trans-evaporation on your skin to keep you cool. If it's hot and you sweat, instead of the breeze instantly drying you off, the cotton keeps the moisture next to your skin, helping it stay cool. This type of dress also protects you from the sun's rays.

But there's a limit to what you can do, and when it gets too hot, it's time to head to higher altitudes.

Energy/Electrical Sources

Few things are more frustrating and disheartening than being in the outback with no power. For some reason, sitting in the dark in the middle of the wilds can leave one with a feeling that you're the only person on Earth. Even just a solar lantern can make the difference between feeling secure and feeling isolated and alone.

Everyone's different in what their power needs are, but we all need lights at night, even if just for an emergency. And some of us want to be able to power up our computers, tablets, cell phones, or even an occasional TV show, not to mention running the furnace and refrigerator.

Your choices as a boondocker are not that many in terms of power sources—you can either run a generator or go solar.

I personally don't like generators, though I can see where they would be handy for emergencies. I had a Honda 2000i that I never once powered up and finally sold, still new in the box. Even the smaller Hondas and Yamahas are noisy, though it's just a matter of degree, and they are quieter than the bigger Champions and such.

Any generator will be heavy, even the small ones, and they can all be fire hazards. They're inconvenient, burn lots of fuel (which you have to safely carry in a can of some type), take maintenance, make your neighbors irritated, and can be unreliable. And they take up a lot of valuable space.

For me (and many others), the best way to generate your own electricity is to use solar panels and batteries. Most serious boondockers eventually end up with solar systems. You can size your system according to how much power you need, and downsize and upsize it as your needs change, simply adding on more panels and batteries.

Solar is quiet, maintenance free, safe, and easy to port around by hand or can be permanently mounted on your rig. The only thing you can't run with solar is air conditioning, and that is bound to change as more people demand smaller AC units that take less electricity.

Whatever you do, never use your vehicle battery to charge things, as the deep discharges will quickly ruin a vehicle battery. You need a completely separate battery system for your rig and daily appliances and gadgets.

So much has been written about solar, and it changes so quickly that any attempt to tell you what you should get would be quickly outdated, but I can tell you what I use.

My first solar system was professionally installed on a brand-new 17-foot fiberglass Casita trailer. I had two portable solar suitcase panels, but the inverter was mounted on the wall and there was wiring that connected to everything so that all I had to do was take the panels outside, orient them to the sun, and plug them into a connector coming out of my trailer.

I had two 90 watt panels, and even though I started camping with that setup in December in Colorado, I never needed but one. Even though the temperatures got down below zero, I always had plenty of power to keep my heater blower going, and sometimes it seemed like it ran all night. I had one AGM battery—these batteries are more expensive than regular RV deep-cycle batteries but can be setup in one's living quarters with no danger of emitting toxic gases or catching on fire, nor do they need maintenance.

My solar panels had built-in converters (which regulate the charging of the batteries), and a 600W inverter (which changes the charge from DC to AC so you can plug in your 110V appliances and gadgets). Be sure to get a pure sinewave inverter if you plant to use sensitive electronics like a computer.

I finally sold that rig and bought another, but this time I went with just one 90 watt solar panel and one AGM battery and a 600W inverter, which had plenty of power for my computer and devices.

I wasn't camping in such extreme temperatures, but it still got cold and this system was fine, though I did notice the times when it wasn't sunny that my battery could get a little low. I eventually went to a 120W panel.

Solar panels are not created equal, and if you're going to be doing a lot of boondocking, be sure to get high quality panels, which typically come from Canada or Germany. Some recommend 6-volt deep-cycle golf-cart batteries, connected in series as this fills both batteries equally, which will give a longer battery life.

Before buying a system, you need to know how much energy you'll need. This is where a good salesman comes in handy, as they will already have a good idea how many amp hours each gadget requires and can size your system for you. It's better to have more power than not enough. A number of really good solar companies are out there, though they tend to come and go.

Installing LED lights in your rig can really reduce the amount of power you need, and as you become an expert camper, you'll learn how much usage you get each day from your panels, including those inevitable cloudy days.

Be sure to check your batteries with your voltmeter and don't let them go below about a 50 percent discharge (usually around 12.1V), as this is very hard on the battery. You can also buy battery monitors such as the Xantrex.

In short, if you want to boondock for very long stretches, you're going to need a power source, and for me, solar is the best way to go. Once you've made your initial outlay, there's no more investment, unlike generators, which always need fuel. And boondocking implies living quietly, which is impossible with a generator.

Helpful Things to Take

Here's a list of items I always take with me, followed by a list of items others swear by. You can combine both lists, but experience will tell you what exactly you will find useful on your own adventures.

It's easier to have something when you need it, but I also like simplicity and not carrying a lot of stuff. Of course, the bigger your rig, the more stuff you can carry.

My list:

General Camping/Boondocking Gear

• A Little Buddy portable heater and several 1# propane bottles for emergencies, a 10# bottle if I'm going to be out long in cold weather. This can be used for tent camping, as well as in a trailer or pickup camper in case your forced-air heater quits working. In theory, you should be able to stay warm for at least two or three nights, giving you time to leave or fix your other heat source, if necessary.

• Several seven-gallon portable water jugs. I will sometimes even carry four of these if I'm going to be out for awhile. A good rule of thumb is a gallon a day for drinking and another gallon for washing. If you have pets, add on accordingly.

• First Aid Kit. I have never needed this and hope my luck holds. Be sure your kit has bandaids, compression tape, moleskin, and rubbing alcohol for bug bites, Benadryl (for allergic reactions or stings), ibuprofin, and a snakebite kit. If you can, add some kind of painkillers.

• I also carry a kit for my dogs that has bandages and compression tape, as well as Rimadyl as a painkiller until I can get them to the vet. I have used this kit a number of times, usually when a dog gets into wire or such. Keep a bottle of hydrogen peroxide if they eat something bad and need to throw up. One of my dogs once drank a bunch of window-washing fluid and the hydrogen peroxide was helpful. My kit also has tweezers (for removing ticks, stickers, cactus, etc.), disinfectant such as Betadine (for cleaning wounds), Epsom salts (for swelling), Benadryl (for allergic reactions or stings), and a digital thermometer. If you need to induce vomiting, it's always best to call a vet emergency number first, as some things you don't want them to throw back up as it may cause more damage than going on through their system. Keep an emergency vet's number in your speed dial, even if they're not nearby. They can advise you what to do.

• Firesticks for my stove and heater. I carry several of these. Bic seems to make a good product. Don't go cheap, as when you need a fire, you want a reliable way to start it. It's a good idea to have some matches for backup.

• Camera (obviously optional, but fun). I also carry a small video camera.

• Handheld digital recorder—I use this for multiple purposes, but it's especially useful for recording info about your campsite for future reference. I also keep a daily journal when traveling telling where I went and what I did, just for my own personal interest. The digital files can be downloaded on your computer for storage and can be fun to listen to later.

• Maps—I prefer having a DeLorme road atlas for each state I go to, as well as smaller fold-out road maps.

• PLB (Personal Locator Beacon) for emergency rescue.

• Solar lantern—you'll always have light, no matter what. An LED battery-powered backpacking headlamp is also very useful as it allows you to do things by light and still have both hands free. It's great for reading if you don't have a backlit Kindle.

• Cell phone—goes without saying, though you may not always have coverage. Some people buy boosters and antennae. Be sure you have a car charger, as well as a solar charger if you're not going to be driving much.

• Extra batteries for your electronics, such as your weather radio (I prefer the crank type, though, as it never needs batteries, but I end up doing a lot of cranking).

• A comfortable lounge chair, preferably an anti-gravity type if you have room. Well worth the trouble and expense, and you can even nap in them.

• A carbon monoxide detector—if you'll be using your heater, this is a safety necessity, even if you're in a tent.

• A propane detector is also a good idea. Keep both in your sleeping area. Carbon monoxide detectors should be kept about waist high and propane detectors kept on the floor.

• Binoculars—a good pair is well worth the price.

• A weather radio. I have a small portable crank-up

AM/FM/shortwave for listening to news that also has the weather bands. I rarely listen to the radio portion.

• Tent and stakes—there have been times when I needed these due to problems with my rig (leaks, etc.), though rare. But sometimes, when pulling a trailer, I wanted to go further back into the bush and this would allow me to take a few days and get way back in where I couldn't get my rig. In addition, it's nice to have for guests and even for staking out your campsite if your rig goes with you into town, as in having a pickup camper. I've had a couple of Paha Que Green Mountain tents and like them a lot, even though they're a bit pricier than some. I would use only an old tent you don't mind losing if you're going to leave it for very long as a camp-spot holder.

• Screen tent—check out the Clam brand name. Easy to set up and very effective and durable. When you're in bug country, a screen tent is worth its weight in platinum, and it seems like when boondocking you're very often in bug country. A good screen tent will allow you to relax without being hounded by bugs and having to spray toxic chemicals all over yourself.

Basic Tools
• Fuses for both your rig and vehicle
• 25' tow strap
• Depending on when and where you travel, tire chains
• A shovel—this will come in handy if you get stuck.
• A fire extinguisher (one for your vehicle and one for your rig)
• A pocket knife and multi-tool

• A good voltmeter

• A good-quality 6x8 foot tarp. These are handy for a number of things, such as covering things in the rain, lying on when under the car, even covering your gear in your car so it's out of sight. You might even want several, as they're cheap.

• Bungee cords

• Bold cutters

• Handsaw

• Pry bar

• Hand axe

• Duct tape and WD-40—if it's too loose, use duct tape; too tight, use WD40

• At least one adjustable wrench

• Spare lightbulbs

• Spare set of fan belts

• A tube of silicone rubber

• Small roll of wire

• Electrical tape

• A good jack and spare tire and lug wrench

• Basic tool set (a simple set of sockets and wrenches, screwdrivers, pliers, hammer, vice grips)

• An extra quart of oil and transmission fluid and brake fluid

• Work gloves

• Backpack in case you need to hike out

• Fix-a-Flat and a portable air compressor, tire plugs

• Jumper cables

• Extra gas cans if you're going out very far

Cooking

• A one-burner Coleman stove. Very portable. I had a two-burner stove and never used the second burner. Be sure to take extra propane.

• A stove-top espresso maker or press, a saucepan for heating water for tea or dehydrated meals, as well as mugs and tea and coffee, of course. I like cream in my coffee, but will settle for other forms of milk (canned, in cardboard, powdered, etc.).

• Stainless-steel pot scrubbers (not steel wool) will scrub your pans clean and also can be stuffed into holes in your rig to keep critters out.

• Freeze dried food—for emergencies, but I've also had these for dinner when I was in the mood for something cooked. I prefer the Mountain House brand. I usually will buy a bucket full of packages, as it's cheaper and easy to store and the bucket comes in handy for other uses.

• A can opener

• One set of silverware and a few bowls

• A couple of kitchen towels as well as paper towels, plastic bags for trash, etc.

Personal Care

• Toothbrush and eco-friendly paste unless you use a trash bag

• Porta potty if you don't have a self-contained rig

• Paper supplies

- Eco-friendly shampoo
- Sunscreen and chapstick
- Good sunglasses
- Shower shoes (flip flops) for taking showers in the dirt and also in motel rooms, etc.

Clothes and Sleeping

- Invest in a good sleeping bag, two would be better. I have a minus zero down bag and one rated to 20 degrees and sometimes combine them when it's really cold. Do not get polyester bags, as they don't breathe and you'll end up wet from your own body respiration. Down is useless when wet, so always keep it dry. A good down bag is worth more than anything else when trying to stay warm, and I prefer Marmot bags, though other brands can be good. Spend extra here and you won't regret it.

- Warm and dry clothing for sleeping are critical when in cold and/or wet weather. I sleep in a warm hat (lined wool is best), longjohns, and warm socks when it's cold outside.

- Invest in some good Goretex rain gear and a good high-quality warm coat. I also carry rain/snow boots, warm gloves, an all-weather hat, and spare clothing. Wool will keep you warm when wet. Cotton won't. Down will if it's treated with something like Gore-Tex.

- Down pillows—I have two high-quality down pillows that make life worth living. Down can be scrunched into various shapes and will stay there, unlike other types of pillows.

- A four-inch memory foam mattress topper. I can use this in my rig for extreme comfort, as well as take it into a motel or B&B room for those beds that are too hard, as I have a bad back.

- Extra sheets. I use these when in motel rooms. I simply drape them across the bed and then sleep in my sleeping bag. This makes me feel clean and cozy and I don't worry if my dogs get on the bed.

- A good sun hat. I also wear a sun neckscarf with an SPF rating when I'm in direct sun for long.

- Really good hiking boots. Don't skimp here. I like Keens.

Recreation

- Books/tablet/Kindle and a small penlight for reading in the dark if you prefer hardcopy books (I use mine to look at maps after dark). I also have a Kindle that's backlit for night reading (the Paperwhite).

- I have an iPad but it's wifi only, so I can't hook up to the internet unless there's a signal nearby. You might want a tablet or laptop that you can connect anywhere. Verizon seems to have the best cell coverage in most of the western U.S.

- Dog toys for playing fetch, frisbee, ball, etc.

- DVDs if you have a power source, card games if you like them

- Your imagination

ID and Important Papers

• Personal ID papers (passport, birth certificate, SS card, medical info, etc.)

• Papers for my pets (vet records, proof of rabies shots, etc.)

• Extra credit cards and cash (well hidden)

• Spare vehicle and rig keys. Some will hide these off-vehicle under a rock or somewhere not obvious so they never lock themselves out.

• A few envelopes and stamps—rarely needed, but sometimes will come in handy.

Pets

• Extra dog/cat food

• Dog/cat brushes

• Dog beds and blankets, unless they sleep with you

• Tie-outs for the dogs, as well as leashes for walks

• Be sure all pets are microchipped (cats and dogs both), as well as wearing collars with tags.

• Emergency vet kit—I had my vet help me put this together, and it includes medicine for upset stomach (pro-biotics), diarrhea, and painkillers, as well as bandages and compression tape. (I also discuss this above.)

Power Source

• 120W portable suitcase solar panel (has a built-in converter) with AGM battery and 600W pure-sine inverter. This provides all the power I need for recharging my com-puter, heater blower, cell phone, etc.

A list of items that others swear by

• Water Purification Kit. The Life Straw fits into a back-pack.

• Hi-Lift Jack and a HenWay

• A Water Thief—a small adapter that allows you to hook your hose to any spigot, even those with no threads

• Potable water hose

• Battery Buddy for jump starting drained batteries

• GPS

• Satellite phone (expensive)

• 7.5 minute topo maps of the area downloaded off the internet

• Full size outside portable table and camp chairs

• Mosquito repellant

• Ham Radio

• Solar Flashlights

• Winch (can be on the front or back)

• 12 volt search light

• Spotting scope for watching wildlife

• Wheel chocks and leveling blocks.

• A broom

• Heavy six-foot locking cable and lock

• Five-gallon solar shower bag

• Bucket for hand laundry

• Some people take a long list of car parts

Conclusion

The art of boondocking is one that is pretty much learned in the doing of the thing, but going prepared makes the doing much easier and safer. Lots of people just go for it, picking up items they need as they go along or making do.

It's really not a difficult lifestyle to learn, though having certain tools and the right rig can make all the difference in whether or not it's enjoyable. And even though this book covers topics like safety and survival, most of it is just simply common sense.

You'll find as you go along that things that seemed intimidating really aren't at all once you're out doing it, and most people you'll meet will be kind and helpful.

So, go prepared, but by all means, go try it out. You won't regret it, as travel and new experiences make our lives richer and give us lots of memories and stories to tell.

So, go make some good memories!

—Sunny Skye

About the Author

Sunny Skye was born in Western Colorado, where her family always went camping, as there wasn't much of anything else to do. She's been RVing all her life, except for time spent going to college and working, and is now an expert on life in the outdoors and the many ways to live well without the amenities of civilization and being in debt.

Sunny now lives full time in her RV with her cats and dogs, campground hosting at various places, spending summers in Colorado, Montana, and Alaska, and winters in Utah.

You'll enjoy her other books, *Living the Simple RV Life*, *The Truth about the RV Life*, *RVing with Pets*, and *Tales of a Campground Host*, available at Amazon.com.

And don't forget to check out the books by Sunny's friend, Bob Davidson: *On the Road with Joe* and *Any Road, USA*.

Cover photo by Sunny Skye.

Made in the USA
Columbia, SC
11 November 2022

70989313R00093